Industrial Law and its Application in the Factory

RODERICK L. DENYER, LL.M.

Barrister-at-Law
Sometime Lecturer in Law, University of Bristol

Macmillan Handbooks in Industrial Management
published in association with the Institution of Works Managers

© Roderick L. Denyer 1973

First published 1973 by
THE MACMILLAN PRESS LTD
London and Basingstoke
Associated companies in New York Dublin
Melbourne Johannesburg and Madras

SBN 333 14330 2

Printed in Great Britain by
THE ANCHOR PRESS LTD
Tiptree, Essex

Contents

5

6

7

Foreword

In the world of modern industry, it becomes increasingly necessary for managers to be aware not only of the fundamental principles of good management, but also of the latest techniques necessary for putting those principles into practice.

Works managers in particular, because of the salient position which they hold in the management structure of modern industry and their responsibility for translating policy into execution, must be both educated in sound theory and trained in modern methods.

This series of eight books has been designed to provide the basis of that education and to supplement essential experience.

I welcome the opportunity the Institution of Works Managers has been given to sponsor this venture and commend the books to all present and future managers in industry.

RICHARD MARSH
Chairman, British Rail
President, Institution of Works Managers

Preface

In writing this book I have received help from many people. From the various personnel managers and shop stewards with whom I have had dealings over the last few years I have learnt to shed, I hope, some of the blinkers induced by a legal training. Tony Dugdale of the University of Bristol has helped explain many things to me and has saved me from errors of which I might otherwise be guilty. He is, of course, in no way responsible for any of the views expressed herein or for any of the errors which doubtless still remain.

My thanks too are due to David Chambers, Derick and Barbara Vann and to my parents, especially my mother who typed some of the early drafts of some of the chapters. The I.W.M. and my publishers have been most helpful, patient and kind, and I thank them. Above all, my thanks to Paulene without whose encouragement the book would never have been completed and who put up with my ill-humour while I was actually writing it.

RODERICK L. DENYER

Guildhall Chambers
Bristol
November 1972

1. | Introduction

The purpose of this book is to explain to the practising manager and the practising trade unionist the way in which English labour law works. The layman confronted with a law book is inclined to 'switch off'. He can hardly be blamed for this since lawyers, especially academic lawyers, have tried to pretend that the law is a mystery capable of being understood only by the initiated few. This is nonsense and the fault lies with us lawyers. Provided the trouble is taken to explain concepts in everyday language, unencumbered by Latin tags, any intelligent layman should be able to appreciate what is going on. This book has been written with the avowed aim of making law comprehensible to the layman. Only the layman will be able to judge whether the attempt has been successful or not.

Because of television drama and the fiction writers, most non-lawyers tend to think of the law as being concerned with crime, that is, that branch of the law which has as its aim the punishment of those who infringe its provisions. For the purposes of this book, the reader can largely forget that branch. Certainly, criminal law is involved in our study of labour law; microscopic fines are imposed on those who breach various provisions of the Factories Act, but, overall, criminal law's impact is minimal. We are concerned with the civil law applied in the civil law courts and in the tribunals. The civil law has as its aim the compensating of people for harm done to them, whether that harm be bodily or financial. A man injured at work is primarily concerned with being compensated for the injury which he has suffered. A man who has been dismissed wants to know whether he can be compensated for his lost wage-packet. This is what this book is all about.

At the very start the dice are loaded against the layman because of the bewildering variety of courts with which he is faced. These institutions are now dealt with first.

11

THE INSTITUTIONS

1. Institutions which might entertain a personal injuries claim

If a person has been injured at work and he believes that this injury was caused by some act of negligence or breach of statutory duty on the part of his employers, he will want compensation. The court in which his action will be brought depends upon the amount of compensation he will be claiming. If the injuries are relatively slight and the total amount of damages claimed is unlikely to exceed £750, then the action will be brought in the County Court. If the injuries are more serious and damages claimed will exceed £750, then the action will be brought in the High Court.

These then are the two courts in which an action is begun. Appeal lies from both of them to the Court of Appeal, and from the Court of Appeal, in certain circumstances, to the House of Lords.

Litigation is, however, an expensive business and most personal injury claims are settled before they come to court.

2. Institutions which might deal with a dismissals claim

Since the passage of the *Industrial Relations Act, 1971,* most claims concerning dismissal are likely to be brought before an Industrial Tribunal. These tribunals are scattered around the country, and may well be familiar to readers because they also deal with claims for redundancy payments.

Should a dismissed employee desire to bring a common law action for wrongful dismissal (see Chapter 3), his claim will be heard by either the County Court or the High Court depending on whether or not he is claiming less or more than £750.

3. Institutions concerned with the Industrial Relations Act, 1971

As the reader works his way through this book he will not be surprised to find that many chapters are more or less dominated by the Industrial Relations Act. The Act has set up a number of new institutions as well as taking over pre-existing ones. The centre-piece of these new institutions is the National Industrial Relations Court (N.I.R.C.).

As with any other court, to disobey its orders and directions is a contempt of court, the ultimate sanction for which is imprisonment. N.I.R.C. has jurisdiction over what might be called the big, collective issues. Large disputes between employers on the one hand and unions on the other will go before N.I.R.C. It is to N.I.R.C. that the Government must apply if it wants to activate things like emergency ballots and cooling-off periods. In addition, N.I.R.C. hears appeals from Industrial Tribunals in matters concerned with dismissals and redundancy payments.

Another agency put on a statutory basis by the Act is the Commission on Industrial Relations (C.I.R.). This is primarily an administrative agency with a wide variety of functions. It is concerned with arranging ballots in those situations in which the Act demands a ballot. It is concerned with formulating procedure agreements and investigating the state of industrial relations in particular plants, firms or industries.

Further, by virtue of Section 121 of the 1971 Act, the Secretary of State 'may refer to the Commission any question relating to industrial relations generally'. In addition, the C.I.R. has to make an annual report outlining the nature of its activities in that year. In other words, its functions are very far-reaching indeed.

The institutions set up by the Act have tried to escape from the sometimes excessive formality which characterises the ordinary courts. Rights of audience are not confined to lawyers and litigants in person. If a person has a case before N.I.R.C. or an Industrial Tribunal, he can get a friend or a shop steward to conduct it for him. Further, if he loses he will not normally have to pay the winner's costs unless the court decides that the proceedings were improper or that there has been unnecessary delay in bringing them.

THE BRITISH SYSTEM OF INDUSTRIAL LAW IN GENERAL

The reader, as he goes through this book, will be struck by the variety of sources from which our labour law comes. Much of it derives from Acts of Parliament. The Industrial Relations Act is only the last of a line of Acts which, at one point or another, have relevance to the workplace situation. A host of Acts and Statutory Instruments govern safety, health and welfare; some of them have general application, while others apply only to particular industries. The payment of wages has long been subject to statutory regulation in one form or another.

Equally important as a source of law are the decisions of the judges. Many of these involve the construction of particular statutes. Many, though, do not. For instance, the law of negligence has been almost entirely developed by the judges themselves. The concept of a duty of care owed by an employer to his employees owes little to Acts of Parliament, yet it is one of the most important areas of the law to impinge upon the workplace. This law, made and evolved by the judges, is what we mean when we talk about common law.

Prior to 1971, however, the core of industrial relations, which is collective bargaining, was largely unregulated by the law. The voluntary nature of the system was the unique characteristic of British industrial relations. At the bottom of it lay the *laissez-faire* ideal that the parties themselves best knew the bargains they wanted to make and, so far as was compatible with public order, they should be free to arrive at that bargain in any way they wanted to. Although professing to bolster this ideal, the Industrial Relations Act has profoundly changed it. We now have detailed legal regulation at the heart of the system, namely legally enforceable collective agreements. We have new rules governing the recognition of bargaining agents and the imposing of procedure agreements upon those who do not have them.

Whether such a development is good or bad is for the reader to judge, but let no one doubt that the change is profound.

Nevertheless, important though the Industrial Relations Act is, we must never forget that it operates against a background of pre-existing law. It cannot be studied in isolation. For instance, there is a well-developed body of common law concerning dismissals. The provisions of the Act dealing with unfair dismissal have to be studied against this background.

Finally, it must be remembered that in a notionally free society, law and order depend in the last resort upon the co-operation and consent of those governed by it. That consent will not be forthcoming unless the law accords in some way with the standards and values of the governed. As he goes through this book, especially perhaps in the chapters which deal with safety, the reader may well feel that the law has not done all that it might to uphold acceptable standards. It is up to managers and trade unionists who are affected by these rules to press for the necessary improvements.

2. The Legal Nature of the Employment Relationship

SERVANTS AND INDEPENDENT CONTRACTORS

It is an unfortunate fact that we must start this book with its most tedious chapter. The layman may well think that the law here diverges widely from the realities of workplace practices; he would be right, but whatever the realities of collective bargaining relationships may be, English law demands that we begin with the individual contract of employment. Any study of English labour law has to start here. Therefore we must analyse this relationship between the employer (conventionally, if archaically, known as 'the master') and the employee (conventionally, if insultingly, called 'the servant').

The basis of this individual employment relationship is the **contract of service.** This contract exists from the moment the employee starts work. It need not be in writing, though certain written particulars of the terms of the contract have to be given within a specified time, this being demanded by the *Contracts of Employment Act, 1963*, as amended by the *Industrial Relations Act, 1971*. The relevant provisions of these Acts will be discussed later in this chapter.

Thus the question that has to be decided at the very beginning of any labour law situation is this: 'When can we say that A is the servant (=employee) of B?' It is vital that this question be answered because from this relationship flow a number of very important legal consequences. These may briefly be enumerated as follows:

1. The employer is vicariously liable for the tort of his employee (see Chapter 8).
2. The employer owes a duty to take reasonable care for the safety of his employees (see Chapter 6).
3. From it, the obligation to pay wages, sickness pay and holiday pay arise (see Chapter 4).
4. It is very important for the purpose of National Insurance.

For many purposes, and especially for purposes of vicarious liability and National Insurance, the employee (=the servant) is often contrasted with the 'independent contractor' employed under a **contract for services**. The employer is not normally liable for the activities of his independent contractor and they are classified as 'self-employed' rather than 'employed' for the purposes of the National Insurance Acts. The attempts to distinguish these two supposedly different sets of persons have bedevilled the law. As Denning L. J. has said: '. . . it is almost impossible to give a precise definition of the distinction. It is often easy to recognise a contract of services when you see it, but difficult to say wherein the difference lies. A ship's master, a chauffeur and a reporter on the staff of a newspaper are all employed under a contract of service; but a ship's pilot, a taxi-man and a newspaper contributor are employed under a contract for services.' (*Stevenson, Jordan & Harrison Ltd* v. *Macdonald* (1952) 1 T.L.R. 101.)

Various tests have been devised for the purpose of discriminating between 'the servant' and 'the independent contractor'. Perhaps the most basic one, and the one most commonly used, is the 'control' test, i.e. has the employer the right to direct not only what is to be done but also how it is to be done? One of the best expositions of this test is to be found in the judgement of McCardie J. in *Performing Rights Society* v. *Mitchel & Booker Ltd* (1924) 1 K.B. 762. Here, the defendants were the managers of the Palais de Danse, Hammersmith. They engaged a jazz band to play for them at the Palais. The band infringed the plaintiff's copyright in a tune by playing it. The question for the court was whether the defendants were vicariously liable for this infringement of copyright on the grounds that the band was their servant. The learned judge said that 'the nature of the task undertaken, the freedom of action given, the magnitude of the contract amount, the manner in which it is to be paid, the powers of dismissal and the circumstances under which payment of the reward may be withheld' all bore upon the solution of the question. However, 'the final test . . . and certainly the test to be generally applied, was in the nature and degree of detailed control over the person alleged to be a servant'.

The fact that X can give orders to Y does not preclude their both being servants; therefore the fact that the works manager can give orders to the foreman, and the foreman can give orders to a particular worker, does not mean that all are not servants of the company. (See *Hedley* v. *The Pinckney & Sons Steamship Co.* (1892) 1 Q.B. 58.)

However, in an increasingly complex technological society, it is clear that the control test cannot, by itself, provide a solution to the problem of who is a servant. In many cases the worker will know far more about a particular process than the person employing him, e.g. a surgeon in a hospital, an electrical engineer or a research chemist. To overcome this problem, other tests have been evolved to be used alongside the control test. One of the most famous of these was that enunciated by Denning L.J. in *Stevenson, Jordan & Harrison Ltd* v. *Macdonald* (see above), which is sometimes known as 'the integral part of the business' test. His Lordship said that 'under a Contract of Service a man is employed as part of the business and his work is done as an integral part of the business; whereas, under a Contract for Services his work, although done for the business, is not integrated into it, but is only accessory to it'. In other words, if the main business of the employer is that of making glass, then those workers who are employed in the factory in the glass production process will be regarded as servants because their work is an integral part of the business; the man who comes every six months to mend the roof will be regarded as an independent contractor – his work is not an integral part of the business of glass making.

Other important indications of the existence or otherwise of a contract of service include:

1. Who has the right of selection?
2. Who has the right to suspend or dismiss?
3. Who pays the National Insurance contributions?

(See *Morren* v. *Swinton and Pendlebury Borough Council* (1965) 1 W.L.R. 576.)

It should always be borne in mind that it is a question of law for the judge to decide as to the existence or otherwise of a contract of service and whether or not a given individual is or is not a servant. He will not be bound by the labels the parties themselves have assigned to their relationships (see *Ready Mixed Concrete* v. *Ministry of Pensions* (1968) 2 Q.B. 497). He will examine all the factors mentioned above and will try to arrive at a conclusion based partly upon the 'economic reality' of the situation.

In spite of these tests, it has to be admitted that they have not enabled the courts adequately to deal with the problem of the nominally 'self-employed' worker. We have only to think of 'labour only' subcontracts and people going 'on the lump'. People who should properly be regarded as employees may, because of the inadequacy of the tests outlined above, still be regarded by the law as 'self-employed'. This means, of course, that the employer escapes many obligations in relation to National Insurance and PAYE, and a worker's right to a redundancy payment may well be prejudiced thereby.

CONTRACTS OF EMPLOYMENT ACT, 1963

It was said earlier that a contract of employment did not have to be in writing. However, by virtue of Section 4 of the *Contracts of Employment Act, 1963*, as amended by Section 20 of the *Industrial Relations Act, 1971*, an employer is obliged to give an employee certain written particulars of the terms of that employee's employment. These particulars must be given within thirteen weeks of the employee commencing his employment. The following information must be included in those particulars:

1. Who the parties to the agreement are.
2. The date when the employment began.
3. The remuneration rate, or the method of calculating remuneration.
4. The intervals at which remuneration is paid.
5. Any terms and conditions relating to hours of work, including any terms relating to normal working hours.
6. Any terms and conditions relating to holidays and holiday pay, any provisions for sick pay, plus any provisions relating to pensions and pension schemes.
7. The length of the relevant notice periods. (See Chapter 3 for a fuller discussion of the notice periods.)
8. The notice must indicate the nature of the employee's rights under Section 5 of the 1971 Act and the effects of any agency shop agreement on those rights (see below).
9. The notice must specify the person to whom the employee can apply when he has a grievance and the manner in which such

application should be made, i.e. it should inform him of the relevant grievance procedure.

SECTION 5 OF THE INDUSTRIAL RELATIONS ACT, 1971

In order to understand requirement (8) above, the purport of Section 5 of the 1971 Act, as well as the nature of the agency shop, must be briefly set out here. Section 5(i) is as follows:

Every worker shall, as between himself and his employer, have the following right, that is to say:

(a) The right to be a member of such trade union as he may choose ['trade union' here means an organisation of workers registered with the Registrar under the provisions of the Act].

(b) Subject to Sections 6 and 17 [dealing respectively with the agency shop and the closed shop] the right, if he so desires, to be a member of no trade union or other organisation of workers or to refuse to be a member of any particular trade union or other organisation of workers [i.e. Section 5(i)(b) extends to both registered and unregistered organisations of workers].

(c) Where he is a member of a trade union, the right at any appropriate time to take part in the activities of the trade union . . . and the right to seek or accept appointment or election and . . . to hold office as such official.

In *Post Office* v. *Ravyts* (*The Times*, 7 July 1972) it was held that Section 5(i)(c) did not confer on members of a registered trade union the right to take part in or conduct reasonable trade union activities on their employer's premises against his wishes. The Act, it was said, did not restrict an employer's proprietary rights in respect of his own premises. It is hard not to feel that this renders this subsection devoid of any real usefulness. It is an 'unfair industrial practice' for an employer to discriminate against or otherwise prejudice a worker because that worker has exercised or indicated his intention of exercising his Section 5 rights (except within the context of an agency shop). A worker so prejudiced may be entitled to claim compensation from his employer; if the employer acted in the way he did because of pressure from some third party, he may be able to claim contribution or indemnity from that third party (see Section 106).

19

THE AGENCY SHOP

As Section 5(i)(b) makes clear, where an agency shop agreement is in force, a worker's rights not to belong to a trade union may be abrogated. Section 6 sets out how the worker's rights may be modified by the existence of an agency shop agreement. It is as follows:

1. Where an agency shop agreement is for the time being in force, a worker to whom the agreement applies shall not have the right . . . to refuse to be a member of the trade union with which the agreement was made unless he agrees to pay appropriate contributions to the trade union in lieu of membership of it.
2. . . . it shall not be an unfair industrial practice for an employer to whom an agency shop agreement applies:
   (*a*) to dismiss, penalise, or otherwise discriminate against any such worker on the grounds that he is not a member of the trade union with which the agreement was made and has not agreed, or has refused or failed, to pay appropriate contributions to it.
   (*b*) to refuse to engage a worker who, if engaged by the employer, would be a worker to whom the agreement applies, on the grounds that he is not a member of that trade union and refuses to become a member of it and also refuses to pay appropriate contributions to it.

An 'agency shop agreement' is defined in Section 11 as follows:

. . . an agreement made between one or more employers and one or more trade unions or between an employers' association and one or more trade unions, whereby it is agreed, in respect of workers of one or more descriptions specified in the agreement, that their terms and conditions of employment shall include a condition that every such worker must either:

(*a*) be or become a member of that trade union or one of those trade unions, as the case may be,

or

(*b*) agree to pay appropriate contributions to that trade union or . . . to one of those trade unions, in lieu of membership, or . . . agree to pay equivalent contributions to a charity [on which see Sections 9 and 10].

20

It will be no surprise if readers now find themselves a trifle bemused. However, it is really quite simple, and the points can be set out as follows:

1. Workers have a right to be unionists (within the meaning of the Act) or non-unionists (within its generally accepted, pre-1971 meaning).
2. It is an unfair industrial practice to refuse to engage someone or dismiss them because they are unionists or non-unionists. The extension of the right to include a refusal to engage is novel. Hopefully it will result in better selection procedures.
3. These rights are modified when an agency shop agreement is in force. Such an agreement can be entered into only by a registered organisation of workers. The agency shop is designed to replace the closed shop; people have either to be members of the union, or pay contributions to the union without being members. If they are conscientious objectors, they may pay the appropriate sum to charity instead.

Finally, to return to the Contracts of Employment Act, Section 4 of that Act makes it clear that each worker does not, in fact, have to be given an individual statement setting out the requisite particulars in full. It is enough if he is referred to a works document, e.g. on the wall of the shopfloor, which does contain the required particulars, and which he has a reasonable chance of reading in the course of his employment (see Section 4(5) of the 1963 Act). It should be noted that Section 4 does not apply to workers who work for less than 21 hours a week (Section 4(10)), and neither does it apply to a worker who has been given a written contract which contains the information which the employer would otherwise be obliged to give by virtue of Section 4.

This then is an outline of that peculiarly English institution, 'the contract of service'. In the next chapter we shall examine some of the incidents normally attaching to this relationship. It has to be the starting-point of many of our discussions in later chapters.

3. | Dismissal

The contract of employment existing between employer and employee may be terminated in a number of ways. It may end by agreement, by notice given by either party, or it may be terminated without notice. It may also be terminated by sickness and other 'frustrating' events.

BY AGREEMENT

This is perhaps the most obvious way in which the employment relationship can be terminated. The parties simply agree that the contract should come to an end. Such an agreement must be genuinely consensual, and the courts and tribunals should be jealous to ensure that no hidden pressures were operating on an employee so as to make him agree to forgo rights which he otherwise held.

BY NOTICE

Either party may bring the employment relationship to an end by the giving of notice. Subject to certain minimum periods laid down in the *Contracts of Employment Act, 1963*, as amended by the *Industrial Relations Act, 1971*, parties can stipulate in the contract what periods of notice they like. It must be remembered that the statutes lay down only **minimum** periods. The effects of Section 1 of the 1963 Act, as amended by Section 19 of the *Industrial Relations Act, 1971*, can be set out as follows:

1. Any employee who has been continuously employed by an employer for more than thirteen weeks but for less than two years is entitled to a minimum of one week's notice.
2. Any employee who has been continuously employed by an employer for more than two years is entitled to a minimum of two weeks' notice.

3. Any employee who has been continuously employed by an employer for more than five years but for less than ten years is entitled to a minimum of four weeks' notice.
4. Any employee who has been continuously employed by an employer for more than ten years but for less than fifteen years is entitled to a minimum of six weeks' notice.
5. Any employee who has been continuously employed by an employer for more than fifteen years is entitled to a minimum of eight weeks' notice.

(Discussion of what constitutes 'continuous employment' is deferred until Chapter 5.)

With regard to the amount of notice to be given by the employee to terminate the contract, if he has been continuously employed for more than thirteen weeks he must himself give a minimum of one week's notice.

It should be remembered that this section in no way prevents an employee from accepting wages in lieu of notice. Further, it is expressly provided in Section 1(6) of the 1963 Act that 'this section does not affect any right of either party to treat the contract as terminable **without notice** by reason of such conduct by the other party as would have enabled him so to treat it before the passing of this Act'. In other words, the common law right to dismiss without notice (or to leave without notice) still remains.

DISMISSAL WITHOUT NOTICE

There are a number of situations which at common law justify an employer in dismissing an employee without notice. We shall now proceed to examine some of them.

1. Disobedience to lawful orders
The early common law position seems to have been that any act of disobedience to any lawful order given by the employer justified the employer in dismissing the employee forthwith. In *Turner* v. *Mason* (1845) 14 M. & W. 112, the plaintiff was employed as a maid by the defendant. She heard that her mother was dying and wanted to see her. She asked her employer for permission to be away overnight, but this was refused. The girl nevertheless went to see her mother and

23

was summarily dismissed. Her action for wrongful dismissal failed, one of the judges (Alderson B.) saying that 'the general rule is obedience, and wilful disobedience is a sufficient ground of dismissal'. The general attitude of the court is perhaps best seen in the laconic remark of Pollock C.B. when he observed during argument that 'if she has a right to go to the death-bed of her mother or father, why not that of any other near friend?'!

It is probable that the common law attitude has now modified itself somewhat. In *Laws* v. *London Chronicle* (1959) 1 W.L.R. 698, the plaintiff was employed by the defendant company. At a meeting, her immediate superior quarrelled with the managing director, and when he rose to walk out, she got up and followed him. The managing director told her to stay, but out of loyalty to her immediate superior she took no notice. She was summarily dismissed, and brought an action for wrongful dismissal. In the Court of Appeal, Lord Evershed M.R. said that in his view it would be going too far to say that the judges in *Turner* v. *Mason* 'laid it down as a general proposition of law that every act of disobedience of a lawful order must entitle the employer to dismiss'. In his view, in order to justify a summary dismissal it had to be shown that 'the conduct complained of is such as to show the servant to have disregarded the essential conditions of the Contract of Service'. In other words, 'one act of disobedience or misconduct can justify dismissal only if it is of a nature which goes to show (in effect) that the servant is repudiating the contract, or one of its essential conditions'. It must connote 'a deliberate flouting of the essential contractual conditions'.

2. Breach of the duty of fidelity

In discussing the nature of the employment relationship, it was observed that the employee owes to his employer a 'duty of fidelity'. This duty to give faithful and honest service comprehends honesty, trust and general 'fair dealing'. It seems probable that breach of this duty justifies the employer in summarily dismissing the employee.

In *Sinclair* v. *Neighbour* (1967) 2 Q.B. 279, the plaintiff was employed by the defendant bookmaker as manager. The plaintiff took £15 from the till for gambling, leaving his I.O.U. He replaced the money the next day after his bet had been successful. When this was found out, he was summarily dismissed. The dismissal was held to be justified! The authority of the plaintiff was a 'breach of the confidential relationship', and the court stigmatised his conduct as being 'on the face of it incompatible and inconsistent with his duty'. In *Boston Deep Sea Fishing and Ice Co.* v. *Ansell* (1888) 39 Ch.D. 339, the plaintiff was employed by the defendants as managing director on behalf of the company. The plaintiff contracted for the building of certain fishing vessels and, unknown to the company, he took a separate (undisclosed) commission from the builders. He was also a shareholder in an ice company which paid bonuses to shareholders who owned fishing vessels and who ordered ice from them. The plaintiff ordered ice for the company, and himself received the bonus. This conduct was held to justify the defendants in dismissing him. The court said that the plaintiff had put himself in a position where his duty and his interest might conflict. Cotton L.J. said that 'where an agent entering into a contract on behalf of his principal, and without the knowledge or assent of that principal, receives money from the person with whom he is dealing, he is doing a wrongful act, . . . and, in my opinion, that gives to his employer . . . power and authority to dismiss him from his employment as a person who by that act is shown to be incompetent of faithfully discharging his duty to his principal'.

3. Incompetence

It is very difficult to say how far the common law justifies a dismissal on the grounds of incompetence. In *Savage* v. *British India Steamship Co.* (1930) 46 T.L.R. 294, Wright J. said that 'an employer was entitled to dismiss a servant for a single act of misconduct or serious negligence. In determining the seriousness of an act of negligence regard must be had, not to the consequences of the act, but to its nature'. It seems that the act complained of has to go beyond 'a mere error of judgement' and into the realms of 'gross negligence'. The words 'gross negligence' are notoriously difficult to define. It may be that one could tentatively put forward a test along the following lines: 'Would a reasonable man, well versed in the requirements and difficulties of this particular job, ever have acted in this way?' The reasonable man will, of course, be subject to errors of judgement. We all make mistakes. To justify dismissal, the conduct complained of must be more than just a mistake: it must be conduct which no reasonable man could have contemplated.

A possible illustration of this point is to be found in *Jupiter General*

25

Insurance Co. v. *Schroff* (1937) 3 A.E. 67 (although this case also contains elements of dismissal for disobedience). The manager of the life insurance department of an insurance company recommended the issue of an endowment policy on a third party, even though he knew that the managing director of the company had refused to reissue the life just a few days earlier. He was summarily dismissed and the question was whether the dismissal was justified. It was held that it was. The court said that 'it can be in exceptional circumstances only that an employer is acting properly in summarily dismissing an employee on his committing a single act of negligence . . . the test to be applied must vary with the nature of the business and the position held by the employee'. However, 'if a person in charge of the life insurance department, subject to the supervision of superior officers, shows by his conduct or his negligence that he can no longer command their confidence, and if, . . . when an explanation is called for, he refuses an apology or amendment, it seems to their Lordships that his immediate dismissal is justifiable'.

COMMON LAW REMEDIES FOR WRONGFUL DISMISSAL

Above have been set out some of the main grounds on which, at common law, an employer could summarily dismiss an employee. If the employee wishes to challenge the validity of the dismissal, his common law remedy is an action in the ordinary courts for damages for breach of contract, sometimes known as an action for 'wrongful dismissal'. Section 113 of the *Industrial Relations Act, 1971*, makes it clear that this common law right still exists, though the section gives power to the Lord Chancellor to make regulations conferring jurisdiction on the Industrial Tribunals in such actions.

The damages recoverable are those earnings which the wrongfully dismissed man has lost. Thus a man who was entitled to six weeks' notice should *prima facie* recover six weeks' wages as damages. But if he immediately obtained a new job at a slightly lower rate of pay, his actual loss is clearly the difference between what he receives and what he would have earned had he not been dismissed, and this would be the measure of damages. Further, the wrongfully dismissed employee has a duty to try to mitigate his loss; thus, he must attempt to find another job and, if he does not take such steps, he will find his damages reduced by some notional amount which the judge thinks reasonable. But the duty is only to take 'reasonable steps'. In other words, a wrongfully dismissed Bristolian does not necessarily have to move to Newcastle to get another job.

It follows from the above that if the employee failed to establish that there had been a breach of contract on the part of his employer, he could not get damages. Further, if the employer had complied with the notice periods required by the contract and the *Contracts of Employment Act, 1963*, it is obvious that no breach of contract could be alleged. Thus, an employer who decided that he no longer liked a particular individual, but who could find no good ground for summarily dismissing the man, merely had to give the proper period of notice. When that expired, there was an end to the matter.

UNFAIR DISMISSAL AND THE INDUSTRIAL RELATIONS ACT, 1971

Section 22 of the *Industrial Relations Act, 1971,* provides that any employee who has veen 'unfairly dismissed' has been the victim of an 'unfair industrial action' on the part of his employer. An employee now has the right not to be unfairly dismissed by his employer. A number of employees are excluded from this protection. The excluded classes are listed in Section 27 of the Act.

1. *Excluded classes of employment*
1. Establishments employing not more than four people, including the claimant (unless he is dismissed for having exercised his Section 5(i) rights).
2. Any employment where the employer is the husband or wife or a close relative of the employee.
3. Employment as a registered dock worker.
4. Any employment under a contract which normally involves employment for less than twenty-one hours weekly.
5. Contracts of employment where the employee ordinarily works outside Great Britain.
6. Where the employee has not been continuously employed for 104 weeks prior to the effective date of termination (unless he is dismissed for having exercised his Section 5(i) rights). (Section 28.)
7. Men over sixty-five or women over sixty, or where before the

date of termination the individual concerned had reached the normal retiring age for an employee holding the position which he held in the undertaking in which he worked (unless he is dismissed for having exercised his Section 5(i) rights). (Section 28.)

8. Dismissal from employment under a contract for a fixed term of two years or more, where the contract was made before the commencement of this Act, and the dismissal consists only of the expiry of that term without its being renewed. (Section 30.)

9. Dismissal from employment under a contract for a fixed term of two years or more, where the dismissal consists only of the expiry of the term without its being renewed, if before the term expires the employee agreed in writing to exclude any claim in respect of rights under Section 22. (Section 30.)

10. A very important exclusion is contained in Section 31. A joint application may be made to the N.I.R.C. by all the parties to a procedure agreement for an order 'designating' that agreement. This means that in cases of dismissal the procedure agreement will govern, not Section 22 of the Act. Before designating a procedure agreement, the N.I.R.C. has to be satisfied of the following matters:

   (a) That every organisation of workers which is a party to the procedure agreement is an independent organisation.

   (b) That the procedure agreement provides for procedures to be followed in cases where an employee claims that he has been, or is in the course of being, unfairly dismissed.

   (c) That those procedures are available without discrimination to all employees falling within any description to which the procedure agreement applies.

   (d) That the remedies provided by the procedure agreement in respect of unfair dismissal are on the whole as beneficial as (but not necessarily identical with) those provided by the Act.

   (e) That the procedures provided include a right to arbitration or adjudication by an independent referee or other independent body in cases where a decision cannot otherwise be reached.

   (f) That the provisions of the procedure agreement are such that it can be determined with reasonable certainty whether a particular employee is one to whom the procedure agreement applies or not.

2. Meaning of 'dismissal'

Before an employee can take advantage of his rights under Section 22, he must be able to show that he has been 'dismissed'. Section 23 sets out that an employee shall be taken to have been dismissed by his employer if:

(a) the contract under which he is employed is terminated by the employer, whether it is terminated with or without notice; or

(b) where he is employed for a fixed term, that term expires without being renewed; or

(c) where the employer has given notice to the employee, the employee gives written notice to terminate on an earlier date; this will still be regarded as dismissal by the employer, provided the employee gives his notice during the obligatory period of the employer's notice, i.e. during that part of the time which the employer is bound to give.

3. 'The effective date of termination'

It is clearly important to know precisely when the contract comes to an end. Section 23 of the Act sets out the dates which are to be regarded as 'the effective date of termination' of the contract, according to the means whereby the contract is terminated. Where the contract is terminated by notice, it means the date on which the notice expires. Where the contract is terminated without notice, it means the date on which the termination takes effect, i.e. if a person is 'sacked' on the spot, that is the time when the contract ends. Finally, where the court is dealing with a fixed-term contract, it means the date on which that term expires.

4. 'Fair and unfair dismissal'

Having decided that a 'dismissal' has taken effect, the tribunal is then called upon to decide whether the dismissal is fair or unfair. This means that the tribunal has to concern itself with the reasons for the dismissal; whether the dismissal constituted a breach of contract is in this context of secondary consideration only. According to Section 24 of the Act, **it shall be for the employer to show** what the principal reason for the dismissal was and that it was one of the specified

29

reasons or was 'some other substantial reason of a kind such as to justify the dismissal of an employee holding the position which that employee held'.

What then are these 'specified reasons'? According to Section 24(2), these reasons are those which are related to:

   (a) the capability or qualifications of the employee for performing work of the kind which he was employed by the employer to do; or

   (b) related to the conduct of the employee; or

   (c) related to the fact that the employee was redundant.

It is further provided in Section 24(2) that the dismissal of an employee **shall** be regarded as unfair if the principal reason for it was that the employee had exercised or indicated his intention of exercising his Section 5(i) rights.

5. The 'redundancy' reason

When the principal reason for the dismissal is redundancy, but it is shown (presumably by the employee) that there existed in the undertaking redundancy circumstances applicable to workers holding similar positions to the dismissed worker and that these other workers have not been dismissed, then the dismissal shall be regarded as unfair if:

   (a) the principal reason why he was dismissed was that he had exercised or indicated his intention of exercising his Section 5(i) rights; or

   (b) that he was selected for dismissal in contravention of a customary arrangment or agreed procedure relating to redundancy and that there were no special reasons justifying a departure from that arrangement or procedure in his case.

Thus we see that (1) it is for the employee to show that he was dismissed, and (2) for the employer to show what was the reason for the dismissal. Section 24(b) then goes on to say that, having regard to this reason, 'the question whether the dismissal was fair or unfair . . . shall depend on whether in the circumstances he [the employer] acted reasonably or unreasonably in treating it as a sufficient reason for dismissing the employee; and that question shall be determined in accordance with equity and the substantial merits of the case'.

Precisely what this last means is not easy to say. It is clearly far-reaching and gives the tribunal a very wide discretion indeed. In the end, it probably boils down to what the tribunal considers to be 'fair' in the particular circumstances of the case. Since individual circumstances vary almost infinitely in their operation, it may well be that what a tribunal considers 'fair' in a particular case will not be of much use in deciding what is 'fair' in another case. Nevertheless, knowing the way English courts and tribunals cling to precedent, it is this author's opinion that very soon we shall have a body of case law on what is 'fair' and 'reasonable' and 'just'. It is to be hoped that this never blinds the tribunal to the merits of the individual case.

6. Compensation

Once the tribunal has decided that a dismissal is 'unfair', it must go on to consider the question of how much compensation is to be paid by the employer. Section 116 of the Act sets out the general principles as to the assessment of compensation. According to this section, the amount to be paid by the party in default 'shall . . . be such amount as the . . . tribunal considers just and equitable in all the circumstances, having regard to the loss sustained by the aggrieved party'. And, by virtue of Section 116(2), 'The loss sustained by the aggrieved party . . . shall be taken to include:

(a) any expenses reasonably incurred by him in consequence of the matters to which the complaint relates, and

(b) loss of any benefit which he might reasonably be expected to have had but for those matters.'

This is all subject to the ordinary rule that a person has a duty to take steps to mitigate his own loss.

On this, as on all aspects of this Act, one hesitates to be dogmatic in ascertaining a meaning. With some trepidation, the following points may be made:

1. Awards are not likely to be high.
2. 'Just and equitable' is clearly qualified by the fact that one must have regard to the loss sustained by the person dismissed.
3. If a person is dismissed on a Friday and starts work elsewhere at the same wage on a Monday, in the absence of things like loss of pension rights or his having to move to a different part

31

of the country to take up the new job, he has clearly, in financial terms, not lost much. How far the tribunal will be prepared to compensate for things like inconvenience, hurt pride, the severing of old associations and the like is anybody's guess. It may be suspected that parsimony rather than generosity will characterise the award.

4. The wrongfully dismissed employee will have to take reasonable steps to obtain alternative employment. This is what is meant by the duty to mitigate.

By virtue of Section 118, the maximum award the tribunal will be able to make to a wrongfully dismissed employee will be 104 weeks' pay or £4,160 (i.e. 104 × £40), whichever is the less. In other words, any earnings over £40 per week will be disregarded. It is obvious then that a managing director on a five-year service agreement at £10,000 per year who is dismissed after one year will prefer to rely on his common law claim for damages for wrongful dismissal, rather than to claim compensation under the Act for unfair dismissal. On the other hand, the unfairly dismissed worker on £30 a week might well do better with his remedy under the Act.

When someone complains under Section 106 to the Industrial Tribunal that he has been unfairly dismissed and the tribunal finds that this is so and it considers that 'it would be practicable and in accordance with equity' for the complainant to be re-engaged by his former employer, it shall make a recommendation to that effect, setting out the terms on which it considers it reasonable that the complainant be so re-engaged. If such a recommendation is made and not complied with by the parties, then, in accordance with Section 116(4), the compensation will be affected. If the reason for the non-compliance is the complainant's refusal and the tribunal finds that he has acted unreasonably in so doing, it shall reduce his compensation. Conversely, if the reason for the non-compliance was the employer's unreasonable refusal to re-engage the complainant, then the amount of the compensation is to be increased.

7. Conciliation

It remains only to mention briefly the functions of the Government conciliation officers. By virtue of Section 146 of the Act, where a complaint of an unfair dismissal has been presented to the Industrial

Tribunal, a copy of it is sent to a conciliation officer. Thereafter, if requested to do so by either party, or where he considers that he could act with a reasonable prospect of success, he has the duty of endeavouring to promote a settlement of the complaint without its being determined by a tribunal. He can try to secure a reinstatement, or, where that fails, he can try to get a voluntary settlement in monetary terms. If he fails, the matter goes before the tribunal in the ordinary way.

SUMMARY OF UNFAIR DISMISSALS PROVISIONS

1. Presentation of a complaint to the Industrial Tribunal under Section 106.
2. Complaint likely to be investigated by conciliation officer under Section 146.
3. If not resolved under (2) above, tribunal has to consider:
   (a) Has there been a dismissal? (see Section 23).
   (b) Was that dismissal 'unfair'? (see Section 24).
4. If tribunal finds that dismissal is unfair, should it recommend reinstatement? (see Section 106).
5. Assessment of compensation (see Section 116).

4. The Payment of Wages and the Truck Acts

WAGES: THE COMMON LAW POSITION

Put simply, in lawyer's terms the consideration for work is wages and the consideration for wages is work: no work, no pay is the rule. This, as we shall see, is subject to varying exceptions. The amount of wages to be paid will be fixed by the contract and set out in that contract or in some collective agreement which covers the terms and conditions of a particular group of employees.

We shall deal first with the situation that arises when, through no fault of his own, the employer is unable to provide work. In *Browning* v. *Crumlin Valley Collieries Ltd* (1926) 1 K.B. 522, the defendants had to close down their mine to enable repairs to be carried out to make it safe. The defendants were not to blame for its being unsafe. Were the employees entitled to wages while the mine was closed? The court said no. It was an implied term of the contract of employment that this sort of risk should be shared.

On the other hand, the position may be different where the fact of no work being provided is the fault of the employer. In *Devonald* v. *Rosser* (1906) 2 K.B. 728, the plaintiff was employed on a piecework basis at the defendant's tinplate factory. His contract entitled him to one month's notice. Because trade was slack, the defendant shut down the works and two weeks later gave the plaintiff notice. The plaintiff claimed six weeks' wages, alleging that it was an implied term of the employment contract that the defendant supply him with work. It was held that there was an implied obligation to provide the workman with a reasonable amount of work and it was no answer to a claim alleging breach of that obligation that the employer could no longer run his works at a profit.

In *Bauman* v. *Hulton Press Ltd* (1952) 2 A.E. 1121, the plaintiff was employed by the defendant as a photographer. Under his con-

34

tract, he was paid a fixed basic amount plus a commission on work actually done. The court had no difficulty in implying the term that throughout the duration of the contract the defendants were bound to give the plaintiff a reasonable amount of work to enable him to earn the commission which both parties must have contemplated he would receive when he entered into the contract.

From these cases we see that the basic principles are: (1) if work is not provided and this is the fault of neither party, then, subject to any express term in the contract to the contrary, no wages are payable; and (2) if work is not provided because of the fault or neglect of the employer, then the wages are payable.

PAYMENT DURING SICKNESS

The position may well be covered by the contract. Where there is no express term governing the matter, it is probable that the wages remain payable. (See *Orman* v. *Saville Sportswear* (1960) 1 W.L.R. 1055.)

THE TRUCK ACTS

The 'truck system', so vividly described by Disraeli in the best of his political novels, *Sybil*, was a system whereby the employer would pay the whole or part of the wages of an employee in something other than current coin of the realm. An attendant evil was the 'tommy shop', whereby the employee was obliged to spend part of what he received (often in the form of special tokens) in a shop owned by his employer. The opportunities for abuse are manifold and obvious. As the culmination of a succession of measures to deal with this problem, the *Truck Act, 1831*, was passed.

The protection of the Act extends to all 'workmen' which, in this context, means all those employed in 'manual' labour. Section 1 of the Act states that all wages should be paid in current coin of the realm and that any stipulation in the contract of employment to the contrary effect should be 'illegal, null and void'. In other words, manual workers are to be paid in cash, not kind. Further, Section 2, which was aimed at the 'tommy shop', made 'illegal, null and void' any stipulations in the contract as to the manner or place in which the money was to be spent.

35

Clearly, this would have the effect of rendering illegal the payment of wages to manual workers in cheques or postal orders. It was to remedy this that the *Payment of Wages Act, 1960,* was passed. This permitted the payment by cheque, money order, postal order or payment into a bank account. The worker must have made a written request for payment by this method, and he is free to revert at any time to the traditional method: it cannot be made a condition of his employment that he accept payment by one of the other methods.

THE TRUCK ACT, 1896, AND DEDUCTIONS FROM WAGES

How far is an employer entitled to make a deduction for bad workmanship and how far is he entitled to fine his employees for misconduct? The position is largely governed by the *Truck Act, 1896.* Basically, the employer cannot fine unless the contract says he can. This can be done by inserting an express written term to that effect in a written contract, or that that term is contained in a notice easily accessible to the employee. In other words, the employee must know that the power to fine exists. He must further be told what acts and omissions carry a fine and what the fine for contravention is going to be. The fine for contravention imposed must be in respect of activities which are likely to cause damage or loss to the employer or constitute an interruption or hindrance to his business. Finally, the fine must be 'fair and reasonable' having regard to all the circumstances of the case. Like considerations apply when dealing with deductions for bad workmanship.

5. | Redundancy Payments

The *Redundancy Payments Act, 1965*, was something of a landmark in the field of legal regulation of employment conditions. Its basic *raison d'être* is to compensate a workman in monetary terms for losing his job as a result of redundancy. Views may differ as to whether the Act was designed with a view to promoting job mobility, to facilitate technological change, or whether it constituted the recognition by Parliament of some sort of 'property right' which a workman has in his job. Howsoever this may be, we are primarily concerned with the fundamental issues like who is entitled to a redundancy payment and when, and if so, how much?

THE PEOPLE COVERED BY THE ACT

Basically, the people covered are those who, at common law, could be called 'servants' (see Chapter 2). They must be able to show that they have been continuously employed in this business for more than two years under a contract of employment which normally involves them in working more than 21 hours per week.

Those excluded from the provisions of the Act are as follows:

1. Men over sixty-five and women over sixty years of age (Section 2).
2. Those under twenty years of age (since weeks worked before the age of eighteen do not count – see Section 8(1) and paragraph 1(1)(a) of Schedule 1 of the 1965 Act).
3. Those who work less than 21 hours per week (see Schedule 1, paragraphs 3 and 4, of the *Contracts of Employment Act, 1963*).
4. Those who have worked for less than 104 weeks with the business or with the business of an associated employer.
5. Where, by virtue of Section 15(2) of the 1965 Act, an individual who works under a fixed-term contract of more than two years

has expressly agreed to forgo his right to a redundancy payment.

6. Where there are collectively agreed redundancy procedures providing for disputes to be finally settled before an Industrial Tribunal, which have been the subject of an exemption order under Section 11 of the 1965 Act.
7. Central Government employees, National Health Service employees, and the holders of certain public offices (see Section 16(4)(*a*)).
8. Registered dock workers – Section 16(1).
9. Shore fishermen.
10. Employed spouses, i.e. the Act does not apply where 'the employer is the husband or wife of the employee' (Section 16(3)).
11. A domestic servant related to his or her employer.
12. Employees who normally work abroad.

Many of these excluded classes will, of course, be covered by schemes for redundancy of their own.

THE MEANING OF 'DISMISSAL'

An employee is only entitled to a redundancy payment when he can show that he has been 'dismissed for redundancy'. The Act has complicated provisions for dealing with what constitutes 'dismissal'. It has nothing to do with the common law legality of the dismissal, though dismissal for redundancy is a justifying reason in the context of unfair dismissals under the Industrial Relations Act.

Section 3 sets out the requirements for a 'dismissal' for the purposes of the Act. A paraphrase appears below.

3(1). . . . any employee shall . . . be taken to be dismissed by his employer if, but only if,
(*a*) the contract under which he is employed by the employer is terminated by the employer, whether with or without notice;
(*b*) on the expiry of a fixed-term contract without its being renewed;
(*c*) where the **employee** terminates the contract without notice in such circumstances that he is entitled to terminate it by reason of the **employer's** conduct.

3(2). For the purposes of the act, an employee is not to be regarded as having been dismissed if his contract is renewed or he is re-engaged by his employer under a new contract of employment and:

(a) the terms and conditions of the new contract do not differ from the corresponding provisions in the previous contract, and the renewal or re-engagement is to take effect immediately on the expiry of the old contract;

(b) where there are new terms and conditions, the offer of the new job is to take effect within four weeks of the ending of the old.

The primary aim of Section 3(2) is to preserve the employee's 'continuity of employment'. Thus, if he worked for five years in a particular business under a contract which was then terminated, but he was offered new employment, in accordance with this section, which he held for a further three years, then, on his final dismissal, he would be entitled to claim a redundancy payment on the basis of eight years' service, all other things being equal.

Thus, Section 3(1) tells us what constitutes a final dismissal so as to interrupt continuity of employment.

THE MEANING OF 'REDUNDANCY'

Having looked at what constitutes 'dismissal', we must now see what the Act means by 'redundancy'. It is an obvious point, but it needs saying, that payment is made only when the dismissal is attributable to redundancy. By virtue of Section 1(2) of the Act, an employee is taken to be dismissed for redundancy if the dismissal is attributable wholly or mainly to any of the following situations:

1. The fact that his employer has ceased or intends to cease to carry on the business for the purposes of which the employee was employed.
2. The employer has ceased or intends to cease to carry on that business in the place where the employee was employed.
3. The requirements of that business for employees to carry out work of a particular kind, or work of a particular kind in the place where he was employed, have ceased or diminished or are expected so to do.

39

So we see that the main fact situations constituting redundancy are:

1. The business has packed up.
2. The business is moving.
3. Certain employees are surplus to the requirements of the business either (*a*) because the number required to carry out existing work drops, or (*b*) because there is a decline in the amount of work which the business is doing.

We shall now examine some of the situations which have been held not to constitute redundancy. In *Hodgkinson* v. *Braintree U.D.C.* (1966) I.T.R. 258, the applicant was the driver of a dustcart and worked for the respondents. He was off work with a bad back and when he reported back he was told that his job had been filled. The evidence showed that the work had not diminished; on the contrary, the dustbins of Braintree were increasing by some 350 new houses per annum. He could not, therefore, claim that he was redundant. (In fact he was dismissed because he was offered another job which he had refused.)

A more complicated illustration is provided by the case of *North Riding Garages Ltd* v. *Butterwick* (1967) 2 Q.B. 56. The applicant had worked for thirty years with a firm, rising to become its workshop manager. He concentrated mainly on the technical side of the garage's business, leaving costing decisions and the like to his boss. In 1965, this garage business was taken over by a larger firm. Mr. Butterwick remained workshop manager, but now he had administrative as well as technical duties. He was incapable of doing these satisfactorily and was finally dismissed, allegedly for inefficiency and incompetence. He claimed a redundancy payment. The evidence showed that he was doing his 'incompetent best' but that he just could not cope. But the requirements of the business had not changed, taking an overall view, even though the requirements relating to the position of workshop manager had. The court said that it was not the position of the individual employee or the requirements of a particular job which were important; what mattered were the overall requirements of the business, and in this case these had not changed.

In other words, the equation is that between the business and its amount of work and not the way it allocates that work between individuals.

In *Hindle* v. *Percival Boats Ltd* (1969) I.T.R. 86, the applicant was dismissed because he was too good and too slow. He did not get his redundancy payment.

One of the strangest provisions of this sometimes obscure Act is Section 2(2). It provides that an employee shall not be entitled to a redundancy payment where his employer would be entitled to dismiss him by reason of his misconduct and does in fact so dismiss him either (*a*) without notice, or (*b*) giving shorter notice than would otherwise be required, or (*c*) by giving notice of full length accompanied by a written statement saying that, by reason of the employee's conduct, his employers would be entitled to dismiss him on the spot. The reader might legitimately ask why this is necessary. If someone is dismissed for misconduct, by definition he is not dismissed for redundancy. The answer probably lies in Section 10, to which Section 2(2) refers. This suggests that the situation envisaged is one where the employee is already under notice to terminate by reason of redundancy and then, during that notice period, does something which would entitle the employer to dismiss him on the spot. In such a situation, the employee may still apply to an Industrial Tribunal for a redundancy payment. If the tribunal considers it just and equitable so to do, they may award him the whole or part of his redundancy payment.

LAY-OFF AND SHORT-TIME

Section 5(1) tells us that an employee is laid off work where he works under a contract which provides that his remunerations depend upon his being given work to do, and he does not get any wages because his employer does not give him any work in that week. An employee is regarded as being on 'short-time' where, in any week, he is provided with work not sufficient to give him half of his normal weekly wages. An employee who wishes to claim a redundancy payment in respect of lay-off or short-time must give notice in writing to his employer indicating his intention of making such a claim. Further, he must be able to show that, prior to his giving this notice:

    (*a*) he has been laid off or kept on short-time for four or more consecutive weeks, the last of which ended not more than four weeks before the giving of such notice;

    (*b*) that he has been laid off or kept on short-time for a series of

six or more weeks (of which not more than three were con-
secutive) within the thirteen weeks prior to the four weeks
before he gave the notice.

When making such a claim, the employee must also give one week's
notice to terminate the contract within certain time limits specified
in Section 7(5) (for which the reader is referred to the Act itself).

Within seven days of receiving the claim, the employer may give a
written counter-notice stating that he will contest liability to make a
redundancy payment because it is reasonably to be expected that
within four weeks the employee will enter upon a period of employment of not less than thirteen weeks during which he would not be
laid off or kept on short-time. If within the four weeks following the
employee's notice to claim he is still laid off or kept on short-time,
it is conclusively presumed that the thirteen golden weeks which lie
ahead will not materialise.

OFFER OF NEW EMPLOYMENT

Circumstances often arise whereby an employee becomes redundant
but is offered a new job by his employer. Is he entitled to refuse that
offer and claim a redundancy payment? This contingency is dealt
with in Sections 2(3) and 2(4) of the Act.

Section 2(3) provides that an employee shall not be entitled to a
redundancy payment if, before the termination of the old contract,
his employer offers to renew it or re-engage him, so that the terms and
conditions of the new contract do not differ from those of the previous one and the new contract is to take effect immediately on the
ending of the old contract. The disqualification arises where the employee unreasonably refuses that offer. We shall pursue this concept
of unreasonable refusal a little later on.

Section 2(4) deals with the situation where the employee is offered
a new job on new terms by his employer. The offer must be made in
writing and the new job must take effect within four weeks of the
ending of the old. The employee is not to get a redundancy payment,
provided that the new job constitutes 'suitable employment' in relation to this employee and provided that his refusal to accept it was
'unreasonable'.

The classic illustration of what does not constitute 'suitable employment' in relation to an employee is *Taylor* v. *Kent County Council* (1969) I.T.R. 294. Here, the applicant had been a headmaster for ten years but had lost his job on the amalgamation of his school with another school. Taylor was offered another employment, at the same salary, in the mobile pool of teachers, i.e. he could be sent anywhere in the county. The court held that 'suitable employment' means 'employment substantially equivalent to that which has ceased' and does not mean 'employment of an entirely different nature but at the same salary'.

We now have to decide what constitutes an 'unreasonable refusal'. This problem applies to both Sections 2(3) and 2(4). It should be noted that, in relation to the latter, a refusal may still be reasonable even though the new job constitutes suitable employment. The best reasons why a refusal is not unreasonable are domestic ones. In *Rawe* v. *The Power Gas Corporation Ltd* (1966) 1 I.T.R. 154, the applicant had worked in the South-east for the respondents for about four years. The job came to an end and he was offered new work in the North. He refused for domestic reasons. He was married, had a house in the South-east, two children, one of whom was still at school, and his wife objected to his going away that far. If he accepted this new job, there was a risk that his marriage would break up. It was held that his refusal of this job was reasonable.

When the new job offered is similar to the old, the refusal may still be reasonable if it involves the loss of a number of collateral benefits (see *Sheppard* v. *N.C.B.* (1966) 1 I.T.R. 177).

It must be emphasised that, although previous cases may be helpful in handling a problem, the solution will always be primarily a matter of fact and degree. All the circumstances have to be looked at.

We have already seen that if the offer is accepted, then Section 3(2) preserves the employee's continuity of employment.

CONTINUITY OF EMPLOYMENT

The amount of any redundancy payment will be dependent upon the length of continuous service which the employee has with the particular business. Section 9 of the Redundancy Payments Act says that a person's employment shall be presumed to have been continuous unless the contrary is proved. In other words, there is a presumption, helpful to the employee, that his employment was continuous.

We shall now examine a number of situations where statute provides that continuity is not to be regarded as having been interrupted.

1. Change in the ownership of a business

In Paragraph 10 of Schedule 1 of the *Contracts of Employment Act, 1963*, it is provided that 'If a trade or business or undertaking . . . is transferred from one person to another, the period of employment of an employee in the trade or business or undertaking at the time of the transfer shall count as a period of employment with the transferee and the transfer shall not break the continuity of the period of employment'. In other words, if X works for A for five years, then A transfers his business to B, and X works for B for a further five years, his period of continuous employment is ten years in all.

Thus, it is important to see what constitutes the 'transfer of a business'. As was said in the High Court in *Kenmir Ltd* v. *Frizzell* (1968) I.T.R. 159, 'In the end the vital consideration is whether the effect of the transaction was to put the transferee in possession of a going concern the activities of which he could carry on without interruption'. In other words, as Lord Denning put it in *Lloyd* v. *Brassey* (1969) I.T.R. 100, has there been a transfer 'of the combination of operations carried on'? If there has, the fact that no goodwill has passed will not matter. Some businesses do not have goodwill, e.g. farming.

The opposite situation, where there is no transfer, is illustrated by *Dallow* v. *Else* (1967) I.T.R. 304. In that case, there had merely been a sale of the physical assets – the fixtures and plant are bought as fixtures and plant and not for the purposes of continuing an existing business. (Under this heading, the reader should also refer to Section 13 of the *Redundancy Payments Act, 1965*.)

2. Paragraph 5, Schedule 1, of the Contracts of Employment Act, 1963

Paragraph 5(1) is in the following terms:

If in any week the employee is, for the whole or part of the week:
(a) incapable of work in consequence of sickness or injury;
(b) absent from work on account of a temporary cessation of work;
(c) absent from work in circumstances such that, by arrangement

44

or custom, he is regarded as continuing in the employment of
his employer for all or any purposes;
that week shall . . . count as a period of employment.

Paragraph 5(1)(*a*) clearly needs no explanation; paragraph 5(1)(*b*)
has been the subject of more difficulty. The leading case is the House
of Lords decision in *Fitzgerald* v. *Hall Russell Ltd* (1970) I.T.R. 1.
Here, the applicant was a welder who had been employed by the res-
pondent shipbuilders since 1958. In 1962, in company with many
other welders, he was dismissed because of a shortage of work. He
was re-employed about eight weeks later in 1963, and was finally
dismissed for redundancy in 1967. In calculating his payment, the
problem was whether he had been 'continuously employed' since
1958 or from 1963. This depended upon whether this eight-week lay-
off was an 'absence on account of a temporary cessation of work'.
In holding that the eight weeks did not interrupt continuity, the
House of Lords said that the position must be looked at from the point
of view of the individual workman. If the employer has no work for
him, then he is 'absent on account of a temporary cessation of work',
even though the business of the employer, taking an overall view, did
not come to a stop. It is the employee's point of view, not the employer's, which is the appropriate way of looking at the situation.

AMOUNT OF REDUNDANCY PAYMENT

I shall deal with this subject only briefly. It is set out in Schedule 1 of
the 1965 Act. The basic provisions are as follows:

1. Weeks worked before the age of eighteen do not count.
2. The maximum multiple which can be taken into account is
   based on twenty years' service. Therefore, if X works for a
   concern for thirty years, it is only the last twenty which
   count.
3. The calculation is based on a reckoning backwards, i.e. if the
   employee is aged sixty, then the years back towards the age of
   forty are the relevant ones
4. The employee receives:
   (*a*) One and a half week's pay for every year of service he puts
       in after the age of forty-one;

(*b*) One week's pay for service put in between the ages of twenty-two and forty-one;

(*c*) Half a week's pay for each year put in between eighteen and twenty-two.

The amount of a week's pay is assessed in accordance with Schedule 2 of the *Contracts of Employment Act, 1963*, which deals with the calculation of normal working hours. Having decided what a person's normal working hours are, the amount of a week's pay can then be assessed.

6. Employer's Common Law Duty to Take Reasonable Care for the Safety of his Workers

THE COMMON LAW AND WORKPLACE SAFETY

Albeit inadequately, the law attempts to protect the bodily security of the workers in an enterprise in several ways. Of these several ways, one of the most important was the idea, developed in the common law courts during the latter part of the nineteenth century and expanded in this century, that the employer owes to each of his employees a duty to take reasonable care for his safety. Breach of this duty which results in injury to an employee gives that employee the right to sue his employer for damages. The amount of damages recovered will, of course, depend on several factors, notably the severity of the injuries and the degree of permanent disability resulting therefrom.

This duty to take reasonable care is, for the sake of convenience, sometimes subdivided into smaller categories. As Lord Wright said in *Wilson's Clyde Coal* v. *English* (1938) A.C. 57, 'the obligation is threefold – the provision of a competent staff of men, adequate material, and a proper system and effective supervision'. However, this list should not be taken as exhaustive. The duty is indivisible. The question is always whether, in any given fact situation, the employer has discharged his duty.

It must always be borne in mind that the duty is only to take **reasonable** care; it is in no sense an absolute duty. What is the standard of care required in any particular situation to discharge this duty is a question of fact, and may vary according to the personal characteristics of the worker involved. The standards required to ensure a reasonably safe system of work may be higher in the case of a disabled than of an able-bodied worker. In *Paris* v. *Stepney Borough Council*, the plaintiff was a garage hand. He had only one eye. His

47

one good eye was damaged during the course of his employment with the defendants while he was hammering out a bolt underneath a car. He was not wearing goggles, and he claimed that his employers had acted in breach of duty in failing to provide him with goggles and were further liable because they failed to see that he wore them. It was not the ordinary practice in the trade for employers to provide goggles for such work. The House of Lords held that he was entitled to recover damages. Lord MacDermott said that 'the employer's duty to take reasonable care for the safety of his workmen is directed . . . to their welfare and for that reason . . . must be related to both the risk and the degree of the injury, . . . the duty is that owed to the individual and not to a class'; therefore 'the known circumstance that a particular workman is likely to suffer a graver injury than his fellows from the happening of a given event is one which must be taken into consideration in assessing the nature of the employer's obligation to that workman'. Put simply, this means that in the case of a one-eyed workman the standard of care required in the discharge of the duty is higher than in the case of a normal, two-eyed man.

In *Qualcast* v. *Haynes* (1959) A.C. 743, the plaintiff was an experienced metal moulder employed by the defendants. Some molten metal spilt from a ladle he was holding and his left foot was injured. He was not at the time of the accident wearing protective spats. His employers had a stock of such spats but had never urged the plaintiff to wear them. The question for decision by the House of Lords was whether the employers were in breach of duty in failing to ensure that the plaintiff wore the protective spats provided. In deciding that the plaintiff must fail, Lord Denning put the matter in this way: 'What did reasonable care demand of the employers in this particular case? This is . . . a question of fact.' His Lordship held that, on the facts before him, the employers had sufficiently discharged their duty by making spats available; they did not need to go further and insist on their being worn. This decision, though undoubtedly right on the facts, has been somewhat unfortunate. Many people have given it meaning which it does not bear. It does not mean that an employer is never, under any circumstances, obliged to see that safety equipment is actually used as opposed to merely being made available. That question is always one of fact. Given the individualised nature of the duty, some situations will still demand that its discharge depends upon seeing that protective equipment is actually used.

Before leaving this discussion of the general nature of the duty, the case of *McWilliams* v. *Arrol* (1962) 1 W.L.R. 295 must be mentioned. It applies not only to the common law duty but to statutory safety duties as well. It establishes the simple, but very important, point that before any successful claim for breach of duty can be pursued, the plaintiff has to show that it was the breach of duty which **caused** his injury. Breach of duty means nothing unless it is the cause of the injury complained of. In the McWilliams case the plaintiff was an experienced steel erector. While working on a particular job, he fell 70 feet and was killed. It was alleged that his employers and the occupiers of the site were in breach of duty, both common law and statutory, because they had failed to provide the deceased with a safety belt. The evidence showed that safety belts had been removed from the site two or three days prior to the accident. This was a clear breach of duty on the part of both defendants, yet the plaintiff (the deceased's widow) failed, because it was found as a fact that even if a safety belt had been provided, the deceased would not have used it. This conclusion was derived from evidence showing that he had never worn a belt in the past. Thus, although the cause of death was the failure to wear a belt, this situation was brought about not by the defendant's breach of duty but by the fact that the deceased never wore a belt anyway. The decision makes some sort of legal sense, but the social wisdom of it may legitimately be doubted.

This then is the background: a generalised duty of care whose particular application depends upon the facts of the given situation. It may be instructive now to examine particular aspects of this duty.

THE DUTY TO PROVIDE SAFE PREMISES

In *Paine* v. *The Colne Valley Electricity Supply Co.*, the defendant electricity company housed its transformers in kiosks. The kiosks were divided into three cubicles which were supposed to be separated by insulating material. In the kiosk in question, the insulating material did not extend right to the back of the cubicle. By virtue of this faulty construction, a workman came into contact with the supply system and received a shock which killed him. It was held that the employers were in breach of their common law duty in that they had not provided their employee with a safe place in which to work. The case is interesting because the defendant company said in their defence that they should not be liable because they had employed competent third parties to supply the kiosks. This was held not to be a good defence. The duty is personal to the employer and he cannot delegate his responsibilities and escape the consequences of any negligence.

In *Latimer* v. *A.E.C.* (1953) A.C. 643, a heavy rainstorm had flooded a factory floor, thus making that floor very slippery. All available sawdust had been put down, but parts of the floor remained uncovered. The plaintiff was handling a heavy barrel and he slipped on an uncovered part of the floor and injured himself. He sued his employers alleging that they were in breach of their common law duty. He said that they ought to have shut the factory down. In the House of Lords, their Lordships said that the question to be asked was what steps would a reasonably prudent employer have taken in the circumstances which here came about. The employers had taken all steps available to them short of shutting the factory down. It may be, their Lordships said, that, in certain circumstances, the danger to the workman is so great that a prudent employer would shut the factory down until the danger had gone. However, on the facts of this case, the employers were not liable for not having taken this drastic step. One had to balance the degree of risk involved of injury to the workman against the expense and inconvenience involved in shutting the factory down. This balancing of the risk of physical injury to employees against the possible economic loss to the enterprise is slightly distasteful. However, so long as we retain a system of compensation based on fault and on foresight of consequences, it will continue to occur.

THE DUTY TO PROVIDE ADEQUATE MATERIALS

1. Tools and equipment

It should always be remembered that the employer's duty is not in any sense an absolute duty; the duty is merely to take reasonable care. This rule was reiterated by the House of Lords in 1959 in *Davie* v. *New Merton Board Mills* (1959) A.C. 604. The plaintiff was injured while hammering a metal drift. A piece of the drift flew off and hit him in the eye. His employer had bought the drift from a reputable middleman, who in turn had bought it from the manufacturers. The manufacturers had given it the wrong heat treatment, which made the drift too hard. However, this defect was not discoverable save by a process which it was not reasonable to expect the employer to carry out. The injured employee sued his employers and failed. The employer was not himself at fault, and the House of Lords refused to extend the notion of vicarious liability to cover the negligence of an ultimate manufacturer with whom the employer had no contractual relationship and of whom he had never heard. The result in this case would have been different had the fault been clearly visible by ordinary examination. The actual decision in Davie's case, though not the principle underlying it, has been overruled by the *Employer's Liability (Defective Equipment) Act, 1969*. This Act lays down that where an employee is injured in consequence of a defect in a tool supplied to him by his employer for the purpose of his employer's business, and that defect is attributable to the fault of a third party, then the injury shall be deemed to be also attributable to negligence on the part of the employer. In other words, provided the defect in the tool is attributable to the fault of somebody, the employers may be made liable for that fault.

2. Protective equipment

We have touched upon some of the problems relating to duties to supply protective equipment in our discussion of *Qualcast* v. *Haynes* and *McWilliams* v. *Arrol*. We have seen that there may be a breach of duty on the part of an employer in his not providing safety equipment, but no liability where that breach of duty cannot be said to be the cause of the injury complained of. We have further seen that it is a question of fact in each case whether the law demands that the employer see that safety equipment provided is actually used. In *Qualcast* v. *Haynes*, the law did not so require. On the other hand, in *Clifford* v. *Challen* (1951) the Court of Appeal said that not only did the employer have a duty to make the recognised prophylactic available (in this case barrier cream to guard against dermatitis), but also a duty to see that, as far as possible, it was used.

COMPETENT STAFF AND WORKMATES: THE PROBLEM OF THE PRACTICAL JOKER

The obligation to provide a safe system of work extends to ensuring that an individual's workmates are not incompetent and as such a potential source of danger to him. This obligation is highlighted and illustrated by those cases where injury is caused because of the antics of the firm's practical joker. The two cases discussed below illustrate rather well the way in which the employer's duty to take reasonable care operates. In *Hudson* v. *Ridge Manufacturing Co.* (1957) 2 Q.B. 348, the plaintiff had been injured by the horse-play of a fellow worker. This individual had gained a reputation over the preceding four years for being a persistent indulger in skylarking activities. This proclivity was well known to his employers and they had warned him about it. In holding that the plaintiff was entitled to succeed, Streatfeild J. said that 'if in fact a fellow workman is not merely incompetent but, by his habitual conduct, is likely to prove a source of danger to his fellow employees, a duty lies fairly and squarely on the employers to remove that source of danger'. In other words, the defendants ought to have dismissed him. Contrast this with the case of *Coddington* v. *International Harvester Co.* (1969) 6 K.I.R. 146, where the defendants had no reason to believe that a particular individual was prone to horse-play. In that case they were held not to be guilty of a failure to provide a safe system of work. In other words, if an employer knows that he has a practical joker on his hands but does nothing about it, he may be acting in breach of his duty. Where he has no reason to know that an individual is that way inclined, he will not, without more knowledge, be found to be in breach of duty.

These then are some illustrations of the employer's common law duty. The fact situations which have occurred and will occur are legion, but always the basic question will be 'Has the employer taken reasonable care to ensure the safety of this particular worker?'

Finally, the effects of the *Employer's Liability* (*Compulsory Insurance*) *Act, 1969*, should be noted. The Act provides (by Section 1(1)) as follows: '. . . every employer carrying on any business in Great Britain shall insure . . . against liability for bodily injury or disease sustained by his employees, and arising out of and in the course of their employment in Great Britain in that business'. And, by virtue of Section 5 of this Act, an employer who fails to insure under the terms of the Act commits an offence. The aim of the Act is to ensure that, should an employee successfully sue his employer for breach of duty, there will be money available to pay the damages.

7. Statutory Provisions Affecting Safety

THE FACTORIES ACT, 1961

In a book of this length it would be both futile and impossible to give a comprehensive account of all the statutory provisions which govern safety in British factories, offices and shops. Here we shall concentrate on the *Factories Act, 1961*, examining in detail one or two of its major provisions. At most, we can aim to show how the courts have tackled certain problems and from this hope that the reader will understand in some degree how the courts set about dealing with statutory provisions affecting safety.

The *Factories Act, 1961*, the latest in a long line of Factories Acts, governs health, safety and welfare in British factories. It is supplemented by a vast body of regulations dealing with aspects of safety in particular industries, e.g. the *Construction (General Provisions) Regulations, 1961*. The Act imposes various obligations on employers and employees, breach of which may give rise to the imposition of criminal sanctions like a fine. However, we are not concerned with the criminal liabilities arising under the Act; our concern is with the workman injured by a breach of the Act's provisions. Such a workman will want monetary compensation, i.e. damages. Normally, his claim for damages for a breach of the Act's provisions will be coupled with a claim alleging negligence against his employer in that the latter was in breach of his common law duty to take reasonable care for the worker's safety. We shall illustrate this discussion by looking at a claim alleging a breach of Section 14 of the 1961 Act which imposes an obligation to fence dangerous parts of any machinery.

THE DEFINITION OF 'FACTORY PREMISES'

Before any claim can be brought, it has to be shown that the *Factories Act, 1961*, did in fact apply to the premises upon which the worker was injured. 'Factory' is defined in Section 175(i) of the Act; a much abridged version appears hereunder:

> ... the expression 'factory' means any premises in which or ... within the precincts of which, persons are employed in manual labour in any process for or incidental to any of the following purposes, namely:
> (*a*) the making of any article;
> (*b*) the altering or demolition of any article;
> (*c*) the adapting for sale of any article;
> (*d*) the slaughtering of livestock;
> being premises in which ... the work is carried on by way of trade or for purposes of gain and ... over which the employer ... has the right of access or control.

Dry docks and transport workshops are also included.

It will be seen from this definition that most manufacturing concerns having as their aim the making of profit will be covered by this definition. In *Stone Lighting* v. *Hay Earth* (1968) A.C. 157, the House of Lords discussed the question of what constituted manual labour. It was held that, provided working with the hands constituted the major part of a person's work, that was sufficient; it did not have to be heavy work, so that a skilled electrician could be regarded as being employed in manual labour for the purposes of the Act, and an electrical workshop could be regarded as factory premises.

It will be noted that, to constitute a 'factory', the persons working there must be 'employed'. In other words, the relationship of master and servant must exist and there must be employment for wages. (See *Pullen* v. *Prison Commissioners* (1957) 3 A.E. 470, where a prison workshop was held not to be a factory.)

THE DUTY TO FENCE

Once it has been decided that the Act applies to particular premises, the occupier of those premises is subjected to the various obligations imposed by the Act. One of the most important of these is the duty to fence. This is laid down by Section 14(i) of the Act which is as follows:

Every dangerous part of any machinery . . . shall be securely fenced unless it is in such a position or of such construction as to be as safe to every person employed or working on the premises as it would be if securely fenced.

Almost every word in this section has received judicial attention. The main problems are as follows:

1. What is meant by 'machinery'?
2. When is machinery 'dangerous'?
3. What dangers must the fencing be adequate to provide against?

1. 'Machinery'

'Machinery', said Lord Reid in *Irwin* v. *White* (1964) 1 W.L.R. 387, means 'machinery which has been installed as part of the equipment of the factory'. In this particular case, the defendants were installing new machinery at their mill. Before all the new machinery had been installed and before it had been put to commercial use, the plaintiff was killed by a part of it which in itself was complete and ready for use. The House of Lords held that the Act applied because this particular machinery was now part of the equipment of the factory.

It follows from this that machinery which is itself made in the factory is not 'machinery' to which the Act applies – it is not part of the equipment of the factory. This was held to be so in *Parvin* v. *Morton Machine Co. Ltd* (1952) A.C. 515.

The fact that a machine is mobile does not mean that it is not covered by Section 14. In *B.R.B.* v. *Liptrot* (1969) A.C. 136, the plaintiff was injured by a mobile crane in a scrap-metal yard. The jib and body of the crane revolved upon a chassis, thus creating a 'nip'. A worker was injured when he was caught in the nip as the crane rotated; it was held that this nip should have been guarded in some way since the crane was 'machinery', within the meaning of Section 14.

2. 'Dangerous'

It is only the 'dangerous' part of any machine which has to be fenced. The word 'dangerous' qualifies 'part' rather than 'machinery'. Thus it follows that there is no obligation to fence a machine if it is dangerous as a whole but has no dangerous parts which can properly be described as parts of machinery.

The basic test of what constitutes a 'dangerous part' was laid down in *Hindle* v. *Birtwistle* (1897) 1 Q.B. 192, where the judge said that 'It seems to me that machinery ... is ... dangerous if in the ordinary course of human affairs danger may be reasonably anticipated from the use of [it] without protection'. He went on to say that 'the contingency of carelessness on the part of the workman in charge of it, and the frequency with which that contingency is likely to arise, are matters that must be taken into consideration'. In another case, *Walker* v. *Bletchley Flettons Ltd*, the judge said that 'a part of machinery is dangerous if it is a possible cause of injury to anybody acting in a way in which a human being may be reasonably expected to act in circumstances which may be reasonably expected to occur'.

This means that the test of 'danger' is basically 'foresight of consequences'. If it is foreseeable that someone is likely to be injured by this part of the machine, then it ought to be fenced. Included among the consequences which are foreseeable is the fact that people are likely to behave in a stupid way. The classic illustration of this is *Uddin* v. *Associated Portland Cement* (1965) 2 Q.B. 582. The plaintiff went into a part of the factory where he was not authorised to go. He was chasing a pigeon and, as the judge said, 'Whatever were his designs towards the pigeon which he was stalking, they were not actuated by benevolence'. He attempted to grab the pigeon and got 'inexorably involved' in the machinery. He presented a claim under Section 14 alleging that it was not securely fenced and he succeeded, though his damages were reduced by 80 per cent because of his own 'contributory negligence'. The Court of Appeal said that 'There is nothing to justify the view that the Act intended its protection for only the slightly stupid or the slightly negligent, and intended to withdraw all protection from the utterly stupid and utterly negligent'.

Thus the fact that a machine actually causes injury is not conclusive as to whether or not it is dangerous within the meaning of Section 14. It has to be shown that there was a **foreseeable** risk of injury. This, of course, limits the scope of the duty.

The danger which has to be foreseen must arise from the use of the machine in the way it is ordinarily used. An employer is not to be held liable for any injury occasioned by the machine going wrong in a totally unforeseeable way. This was decided in *Eaves* v. *Morris*

56

Motors (1961) 2 Q.B. 385. This case also decided that the fact that a part of a machine is not dangerous when it is empty is irrelevant; what matters is whether it is dangerous when doing its normal job, even if it only becomes dangerous by virtue of the juxtaposition of the workpiece and the part (see *Callow* v. *Johnson* (1971) A.C. 335). Once it has been decided that a part of machinery is dangerous, then, in the language of the lawyer, the duty to fence is said to be absolute. This means that the dangerous part must be fenced even though that fencing would thereby render the machine useless from an operational point of view. This was decided in *Summers* (*John*) v. *Frost* (1955) A.C. 740. Here the injured workman was using a power-driven grindstone. The back and top of the grinding wheel was fenced, only a small area needed for the actual grinding remained unfenced, and it was at this point that the man was injured. He brought an action alleging breach of the duty to fence. The defendant employers pointed out that the machine was guarded as far as was practicable to allow it to be used at all. The House of Lords expressed great sympathy with this view but said that the duty was absolute: this was a dangerous part and had to be fenced regardless of the consequences.

3. Dangers the fencing is required to provide against

The cases decide that the basic obligation imposed by the duty to fence is to keep the operator out and not the dangerous part in. In *Nicholls* v. *F. Austin Ltd* (1946) A.C. 493, a woman was injured while operating a circular saw when a piece of wood flew out of the machine and hurt her. It was held that Section 14 did not extend to guarding against dangerous materials being ejected from the machine. The aim of the section is to shield the dangerous part so as to prevent the operator's body coming into contact with it. This is so whether it is a piece of the machine itself which is thrown out or a piece of material on which the machine was working (see *Close* v. *Steel Co. of Wales Ltd* (1962) A.C. 367).

Although there may be no remedy under Section 14 for a person injured by materials being ejected, he may still have a cause of action at common law for negligence. This would be so where it could be shown that the machine had frequently in the past behaved in this way, but the employers had taken no steps to counteract the danger.

The position outlined above has been rendered even more absurd by the decision of the House of Lords in *Sparrow* v. *Fairey Aviation*

Co. Ltd (1964) A.C. 1019. It was held that the duty to fence did not extend to guarding against the possibility that a tool which the operator was using might come into contact with a dangerous part. However, it seems likely that the duty does extend to preventing operatives' clothes from being caught in such a part.

4. *Miscellaneous*

It will be noted that the obligation is to fence 'securely'. Fencing is secure when it effectively prevents the worker from coming into contact with the dangerous part. This does not mean that it has to be secure against all assaults by foolhardy individuals bent on dispensing with the fencing at all costs.

By virtue of Section 16 of the 1961 Act, the fencing provided 'shall be of substantial construction and constantly maintained and kept in position while the parts required to be fenced . . . are in motion or use'. It will come as no surprise to readers to find that the words 'in motion or use' have given rise to great difficulty. It is clear that a part can be 'in motion' even when it is not 'in use'. The word 'use' clearly refers to the machine doing the job it is meant to do and being operated for that purpose. Whether the part required to be fenced is 'in motion' will depend upon: (1) why it is moving; (2) how fast it is moving; (3) the duration of the movement. Mercifully, in the normal run of things a commonsense view of the words will suffice.

The requirement that the fencing must be kept in position does not apply when such dangerous parts 'are necessarily exposed for examination and for any lubrication or adjustment shown by the examination to be immediately necessary'.

This then is a very general outline of the duty to fence. It is, perhaps necessarily, somewhat complex and technical. The requirements can be summarised as follows:

1. The duty is only to fence dangerous parts.
2. A part is dangerous when it is a foreseeable source of injury.
3. Once a part has been shown to be dangerous, then it must be fenced, even though the machine would thereby be rendered inoperative.
4. The fencing must be kept in position all the while the machine is in motion or use.

5. It must be adequate to protect the careless and inattentive as well as the careful and diligent – which does not include the man determined to get inside the machine at all costs.

In order to succeed in an action for breach of statutory duty, the plaintiff has merely to show that there was a breach of the relevant regulation and that he has been injured by it. Thereafter, it is up to the employer to show that the breach was in no way due to his fault or the fault of someone for whom he is responsible. In other words, he has to show that the breach occurred solely because of the actions of the injured plaintiff, for example because he deliberately dismantled the fencing. The question is always 'Whose fault was it?', and if the fault was entirely that of the plaintiff, then he cannot recover. If both are to blame, then the plaintiff will succeed but his damages will be reduced in proportion to the amount the court finds him responsible.

8. | Vicarious Liability

We now come to one of the most important topics in this book, that of vicarious liability. An employer will be liable for the **tortious** (=wrongful at civil law) acts of his employees committed by them in the course of their employment; hence 'vicarious liability'. Thus, the employer himself need not have been 'at fault'. The 'fault' is that of the employee. The justification for making the employer liable is largely social and economic. An employee who injures me is unlikely to be able to compensate me for any harm I might suffer. He has not got the money but his employer's insurance company has. All employers are compelled by virtue of the *Employer's Liability (Compulsory Insurance) Act, 1969*, to insure against this form of liability. The premium is merely one of the costs of the enterprise; it is a reasonable cost for the enterprise to bear because, after all, the injured person is, in reality, complaining that he has been harmed by the activities of that enterprise.

FOR WHOSE ACTS IS THE EMPLOYER LIABLE?

As a general rule, the employer is liable only for the tort of his servant; he is not liable for what his independent contractor does except in special instances. We have already discussed the difference between servants and independent contractors. We have seen the difficulties which attend attempts to differentiate them, and we shall not pursue the matter further.

WHEN IS THE EMPLOYER LIABLE?

1. Act authorised by the employer
Where the servant has been told to do a specific thing by his employer and that involves the employee acting in breach of some duty owed by him, the employer will clearly be liable. This is obvious and need not be discussed further.

2. Servant doing wrongfully that which he is employed to do

The employer will be liable where the servant is doing that which he is employed to do, albeit that he does it negligently. It will be otherwise where the servant is doing something totally different from that which he is employed to do. A couple of illustrations may clarify this.

In *Century Insurance Co.* v. *N.I.R.T.B.* (1942) A.C. 509, an employee was employed to drive a petrol tanker and deliver petrol to his employer's customers. One day, while transferring petrol from the tanker to a storage tank, he lit up a cigarette and threw away the match. Inevitably, an explosion ensued and the question was whether his employers were liable for his undoubted negligence. The House of Lords had no hesitation in deciding that they were. The employee was doing that which he was employed to do, namely deliver petrol. The fact that he did it negligently was neither here nor there. He was still acting within the course of his employment.

An employer may be liable for dishonest acts committed by his servant provided that the servant is acting within the scope of his employment, i.e. doing dishonestly that which he is employed to do. This is so even where the dishonest act is done entirely for the benefit of the servant and in no way for his employer's benefit. In *Lloyd* v. *Grace, Smith & Co.* the defendants were a firm of solicitors. They employed a managing clerk who conducted their conveyancing business without supervision. The plaintiff was a widow who owned some cottages. She went to the defendants' office where she saw the managing clerk. He induced her to give him instructions to sell the cottages and to sign two documents which he told her were necessary for the sale but which were in fact a conveyance of the cottages to himself. He then disposed of the property for his own benefit. The defendants, who had in no way benefited, were held liable to reimburse the plaintiff for their managing clerk's fraud. The clerk was doing that which he was employed to do, but was doing it dishonestly.

3. Servant acting totally outside the scope of his employment

Where the servant injures someone in the course of doing something totally different from that which he was employed to do, his employer will not be liable. The employee is 'off on a frolic of his own' and his employer cannot be held responsible for that. In *Hilton* v. *Thomas Burton (Rhodes) Ltd* (1961) 1 W.L.R. 705, the plaintiff's husband was one of a group of demolition workers who had the use of a firm's van to travel to and from work. On the day in question they had done very little work, but had used the van for several journeys to a public house a few miles away. On their way back from the pub the plaintiff's husband was killed because of the negligence of the van driver. The employers were held not to be liable for this negligence. The employees were none of them acting within the scope of their employment but were going about their own affairs in their employer's time.

This then is a simplified account of the doctrine of vicarious liability. It applies not only when an employee injures some person who has no connection with the enterprise but also when one servant negligently injures a fellow servant. Suppose an employee has negligently spilled some oil on a workshop floor and a few minutes later a fellow worker comes along and slips over that oil. The employer will be liable to him for the negligence of the oil-spiller (in addition to other possible liabilities both at common law and under the *Factories Act, 1961*).

It remains to point out that where an employer has been held vicariously liable for some injury done by his employee to someone else, he can, at law, claim an indemnity from his negligent employee for what he has paid out. This was decided in the controversial case of *Lister* v. *Romford Ice Co.* (1957) A.C. 555. Here, the appellant, in the course of his employment by the respondents as a lorry driver, negligently knocked down his mate (who happened to be his father). The father successfully sued the respondents as being vicariously liable for the negligence of his son. The respondents now claimed an indemnity from the son, alleging that he was in breach of some implied term in his contract of employment that he would use reasonable care and skill in his employment. The House of Lords upheld this claim. Viscount Simonds, in what one can only describe as a quite amazing passage, said:

The common law demands that the servant should exercise his proper skill and care in the performance of his duty; the graver the consequences of any derelictions, the more important it is that the sanction which the law imposes should be maintained. That sanction is that he should be liable in damages to his master; . . . to grant the servant immunity from such an action would tend to create a feeling of irresponsibility in a class of person from whom, perhaps more than any other, constant vigilance is owed to the community.

Whole vistas of an unrealistic new form of liability opened up, namely that of an obligation on the part of an employee to indemnify his employer for the consequences of his negligence, against which the employer is, of course, insured. Subsequently, a gentleman's agreement was entered into by the various insurance companies to the effect that they would not enforce their rights of subrogation on an employer's liability policy to claim this indemnity.

9. | Contributory Negligence and Damages

CONTRIBUTORY NEGLIGENCE

We have now looked at the employer's common law duties towards his employees with regard to their safety, his statutory duties and his vicarious liability. All of them, somewhere along the line, involve 'fault' on the part of the employer or someone for whom he is responsible. It follows, then, that he should be responsible for compensating an injured workman only to the extent that he is at 'fault'. Any part of the injuries caused by the workman himself are the workman's own responsibility. The law recognises this by the concept of contributory negligence. An injured person's damages are to be scaled down by the amount which he himself is to blame for the accident. This position is a result of the *Law Reform (Contributory Negligence) Act, 1945*. It is not proposed to deal with this in detail; suffice it to say that, depending on the degree of fault of the plaintiff, his damages may be reduced by anything up to 100 per cent.

It may be observed, in passing, that many people, including the author, feel that the whole concept of 'fault' in the context of industrial accidents is now totally outdated. Various alternatives have been suggested; this author feels that a national insurance system along the lines of the *National Insurance (Industrial Injuries) Act, 1965*, is perhaps the answer. The amount of compensation would be wholly determined by the amount of injury suffered, thus rendering unnecessary long inquiries directed at establishing 'fault' on the part of somebody.

DAMAGES

Damages have as their aim the compensation of the person injured, not the punishment of the wrongdoer. Roughly, how much you get depends on how badly you were injured. Among the items recoverable as damages, we may include the following:

1. Loss of earnings
If as a result of an injury a person is off work for three months, he is entitled to claim for those three months' loss of earnings.

2. Loss of future earnings
If as a result of the accident a person is incapable of going back to his previous employment but has to take lower-paid, less strenuous employment, he is entitled to be compensated for that fact. The same applies where he is totally incapacitated in so far as work is concerned. The court normally takes his previous yearly earnings and multiplies it by x number of years, depending upon various factors like the age of the injured worker. The multiple is very rarely more than sixteen years.

3. Pain and suffering and loss of expectation of life
These also are factors which the court has to take into account.

10. Collective Bargaining and the Legal Enforceability of Collective Agreements

Traditionally, the approach of English law to collective bargaining and collective agreements was to let the parties get on with it themselves. The legal framework was minimal. The generally accepted view was that collective agreements themselves were not legally enforceable contracts, a view which was confirmed in *Ford Motor Co.* v. *A.E.F.* (1969) 2 Q.B. 303. Much of this has now been changed by the *Industrial Relations Act, 1971.*

DEFINITION OF 'COLLECTIVE AGREEMENT'

In Section 166, the 1971 Act sets out to define a collective agreement. The definition is both long and difficult to understand. It may be paraphrased thus:

An agreement or arrangement made by or on behalf of one or more organisations of workers with one or more employers or employers' organisations, which prescribes the terms and conditions of employment of one or more descriptions of workers *or* which deals with any of the matters to which a procedure agreement can relate.

A procedure agreement can relate to any of the following matters:

1. Machinery for consultation with regard to terms and conditions of employment *or* machinery for the settlement by negotiation or arbitration of terms and conditions of employment.
2. Machinery for consultation, negotiation or arbitration with regard to other problems which arise between employers and workers.

3. Parts of agreements which deal with negotiating rights.
4. Parts of agreements which deal with facilities provided for workers' representatives.
5. Procedures relating to dismissals and matters of discipline other than dismissal.
6. Grievance procedures.

This definition clearly covers most of the areas of industrial relations which are likely to be the subject of agreements. Nevertheless, it is important at the very outset to be able to see whether any agreement or arrangement is a collective agreement within the meaning of the Act, since all the other provisions depend upon that. To these we now turn.

EFFECT OF COLLECTIVE AGREEMENT

By Section 34 of the Act, every collective agreement made in writing after the commencement of the Act shall be **conclusively presumed** to have been intended by the parties to be a legally enforceable contract, unless it is stated in the agreement that it is not intended to be legally enforceable. Further, if the 'opting out' clause is only expressed to apply to part of the agreement, the rest is presumed to be binding. In other words, by saying nothing, you risk a legally enforceable agreement.

A rather more intricate provision, dealing with the proceedings of voluntary joint negotiating bodies, is set out in Section 35. A 'joint body' for the purposes of this section is one that consists of representatives of one or more organisations of workers and one or more employers or organisations of employers, established by or under a collective agreement for either or both of the following purposes:

1. Regulating the terms and conditions of employment of workers of one or more descriptions.
2. Determining, in relation to workers of one or more descriptions, any matters for which a procedure agreement can provide (for which, see Section 166).

With regard to such joint bodies, it is conclusively presumed that the parties represented on it intended to authorise it to make agreements having effect as legally enforceable contracts on all matters falling within the scope of its authority. This does not mean that every decision it makes takes effect as a legally enforceable agreement; what it does mean is that if any dispute arises as to whether or not any decision is legally binding, no one represented on the joint body can turn round and say that they never intended their representative to have the power to make any agreement binding on them.

Any decision made by such a joint body on a matter falling within the scope of its authority is conclusively presumed to be intended to take effect as a legally enforceable contract, provided that the decision is recorded in writing and provided that there is no provision stating that it is not intended to be legally binding. This means that a decision of the local works committee recorded in the minutes will be legally binding unless there is an express written clause stating otherwise.

BREACH OF COLLECTIVE AGREEMENT

By virtue of Section 36 of the 1971 Act, it is an 'unfair industrial practice' for any party to a legally enforceable collective agreement to break that agreement. Further, it is an unfair industrial practice for any party to any such agreement not to take all such steps as are reasonably practicable for the purposes of:

1. Preventing persons purporting to act on behalf of that party from taking any action which contravenes any undertaking given by that party and contained in the agreement.
2. Securing that such action is not continued and that further action will not occur.

For example, if a specific 'no strikes' pledge had been given by a union in a legally enforceable collective agreement and a small group of workers who were members of that union took action involving a breach of that pledge, the union itself would be guilty of an unfair industrial practice unless it took all reasonable steps to put an end to that action. It is a moot point whether 'all reasonable steps' extends to expelling these men from the union; this author feels that it might, given the approach of the courts to the problem of official union authority shown in *Heaton's Transport* v. *Transport and General Workers' Union* (1972) 3 W.L.R. 431.

REMEDY FOR BREACH OF LEGALLY ENFORCEABLE COLLECTIVE AGREEMENT

A complaint may be presented to the National Industrial Relations Court (N.I.R.C.) under Section 101 of the Act that action has been taken by a party to a legally enforceable collective agreement and that that action constitutes an unfair industrial practice on his part in that it involves a breach of the agreement.

If N.I.R.C. finds that the complaint is well founded, it may, where it considers that it would be 'just and equitable' to do so, grant any one or more of the following remedies as it considers appropriate:

1. A declaration setting out the rights of the parties in relation to the matter which is the subject of complaint.
2. An award of compensation.
3. An injunction (though it is not called this in the Act). This calls upon the wrongdoer to stop doing the wrongful act and not to do anything similar in the future. Disobedience to this order would, of course, constitute contempt of court, the ultimate penalty for which is imprisonment.

The amount of compensation ordered to be paid will be such an amount as the court considers just and equitable in all the circumstances, having regard to the loss sustained by the aggrieved party. Further, if the court finds that the aggrieved party was himself partly to blame for the state of affairs about which he is claiming, then the court may reduce his compensation (see Section 116). Section 117 sets out certain limitations on the amount of compensation which can be awarded against a trade union. It must be remembered that we are here talking about 'trade unions' within the meaning of the Act, i.e. bodies registered under the Act. The limitations as to amount are as follows:

1. Membership of less than 5,000 – limit £5,000.
2. Membership of 5,000–25,000 – limit £25,000.
3. Membership of 25,000–100,000 – limit £50,000.
4. Membership of more than 100,000 – limit £100,000.

Subject to one important exception, these limitations do not apply to unregistered organisations of workers. That exception is set out in

Section 154(4) of the Act, which says that no award of compensation can be enforced out of any funds held by that organisation if, under the rules of that organisation, that fund cannot be used for financing strikes or other industrial action. This, of course, is only an indirect limitation: the court can award what it likes, but the successful party cannot get his hands on that fund.

THE ACT AND NON-EXISTENT OR DEFECTIVE PROCEDURE AGREEMENTS

Many industries and plants have detailed and well-thought-out procedure agreements governing a wide range of matters. Ideally, they should not be ambiguous and they should be capable of speedy application. Unfortunately many do not live up to this ideal and, further, some concerns may well have nothing which remotely resembles a procedure agreement. Sections 37 to 43 of the Act attempt to deal with this situation. The provisions are complicated, so readers must show forbearance.

Section 37 states that certain people may make an application to N.I.R.C. with respect to a particular unit of employment on the ground that the unit suffers from one or both of the following defects:

1. The absence of any, or any suitable, procedure agreement for the settling of disputes and grievances promptly and fairly.
2. Where a procedure agreement is in existence, there has been recourse to industrial action contrary to the terms or intentions of that agreement.

It should be noted that 'a unit of employment' means an undertaking or part of an undertaking.

The people who may make an application under this section are the following:

1. The Secretary of State for Employment.
2. The employer.
3. Any trade union whom the employer recognises as having negotiating rights in respect of that unit of employment.
4. Any trade union which is a party to any existing procedure agreement which relates to that unit.

Before the Secretary of State makes his application he must consult with the various parties concerned. Before any other party makes an application they must give notice to the Secretary of State of their intention to make the application. The Secretary of State must then attempt to promote an agreement between the parties without their having the necessity of recourse to N.I.R.C. If this fails, then the application goes forward to N.I.R.C.

If it appears to N.I.R.C. that the unit of employment does suffer from one of the defects set out above, and that because of that the development or maintenance of orderly industrial relations in that unit has been seriously impeded or there have been substantial and repeated losses of working time, then it is to refer the whole question to the Commission on Industrial Relations (C.I.R.). The C.I.R. is then to investigate whether in fact those defects exist and what remedy (if any) is to be recommended.

If the C.I.R. decides that such defects do exist and that new proposals are to be formulated, it has first to decide to what size of unit the new proposals are to apply, i.e. to the unit mentioned in the original application or some larger unit. N.I.R.C. may give effect to this recommendation by ordering that any new proposals should apply to the larger unit.

Having sorted out the question of the size of the unit to be affected, the C.I.R. then has to consider who should be the parties to any new procedure agreement. Basically, they are to be those who are party to any existing procedure agreement and those who would be appropriate parties to any new agreement.

The C.I.R. then attempts to promote discussion between the parties with a view to obtaining their agreement about new provisions, those provisions being so formulated as to be capable of taking effect as a legally enforceable contract. If agreement is then obtained, N.I.R.C., on the advice of the C.I.R., may withdraw the matter.

Where the matter is not so withdrawn, the C.I.R. is to prepare a report setting out the new provisions which in its view are required, these new provisions being formulated in such a way as to be capable of taking effect as a legally enforceable agreement. This report is then sent back to N.I.R.C. At any time within the six months following N.I.R.C.'s receiving this report, any employer or trade union specified as a party may apply for an order directing that the proposals take effect as the procedure agreement for that relevant unit and specifying the parties upon whom that agreement is to be binding. When N.I.R.C. makes such an order, the provisions take effect as a legally enforceable contract.

The moral of all this is obvious. Put your procedure agreements in order, otherwise you may find imposed upon you an agreement which is legally enforceable, breach of which involves an unfair industrial practice.

THE SOLE BARGAINING AGENT

In its infatuation with foreign systems of legal regulation of industrial relations, the Act has imported a number of terms and ideas not indigenous to either British law or British industrial relations. One of these is the notion of the **bargaining unit** and the **sole bargaining agent**. A 'bargaining unit' is defined in Section 44 as being 'those employees . . . of an employer or of two or more associated employers, in relation to whom collective bargaining . . . is, or could appropriately be, carried on by an organisation of workers or a joint negotiating panel'. A 'sole bargaining agent' in relation to a bargaining unit means the organisation of workers or joint negotiating panel having negotiating rights in relation to that unit to the exclusion of all other organisations.

In the past, battles have often been fought over the question of recognition of a particular organisation of workers to have negotiating rights in relation to particular units. The provisions of the Act dealing with recognition of sole bargaining agents are an attempt to settle recognition disputes through the mechanism of the law.

The procedure for dealing with this problem is set out in Section 45. An application may be made to N.I.R.C. for them to refer the following two questions to the C.I.R. for examination:

1. Whether a specified group of employees should be recognised by their employer as a bargaining unit or whether that group should be regarded as comprising separate bargaining units.
2. Whether, for any such bargaining unit, a sole bargaining agent should be recognised and, if so, which organisation of workers or joint negotiating panel should be recognised.

The application to N.I.R.C. under this section may be made by any of the following:

1. By one or more trade unions.
2. By the employer or employees.
3. By the employer jointly with any trade union.
4. By the Secretary of State.

Prior to the application, all the applicants (other than the Secretary of State) have to give notice of their intention to apply to the Secretary of State. The Secretary of State must then endeavour to promote a settlement of the matter by agreement.

Provided N.I.R.C. is satisfied that the parties have endeavoured to reach a negotiated settlement and have used the conciliation facilities open to them, it must refer the question to the C.I.R. provided it is satisfied that this will help promote a satisfactory settlement of the question.

The ball now being firmly in the C.I.R.'s court, it is up to them to prepare a report setting out their recommendations (see Section 48). That report is to be sent to N.I.R.C., the relevant parties are to get a copy, and it is to be published. In the course of preparing this report and in considering what recommendations to make, the C.I.R. must consider the extent to which employees in the group covered by the reference have interests in common, paying special regard to:

1. The nature of the work which they are employed to do.
2. Their training, experience and qualifications.

In other words, it has to be seen whether there is a sufficient identity of interest between particular workers to enable them to be meaningfully regarded as a 'bargaining unit'.

Before recommending that an organisation of workers be recognised as a sole bargaining agent, the C.I.R. has to be satisfied as to the following matters:

1. That the organisation is an independent organisation of workers. (This should end any fear that this particular part of the Act will encourage 'company unions'.)
2. That the recognition of this organisation as sole bargaining agent for the bargaining unit would be in accordance with the general wishes of the employees comprised in that unit, and would promote a satisfactory and lasting settlement of the questions in issue.

3. Whether the organisation in question has or would have the support of a substantial proportion of the employees comprised in the bargaining unit.
4. Whether the organisation has the resources and is so organised as to enable it effectively to represent the employees comprised in the unit.

Further, the C.I.R. may lay down certain conditions to be complied with by the organisation as a condition of their being recommended as bargaining agent, including a condition that the organisation make available sufficient trained officials for the purposes of collective bargaining.

When the C.I.R. has recommended to N.I.R.C. that a particular organisation of workers be recognised as sole bargaining agent for a particular unit, then any of the following may make an application to N.I.R.C. for it to order the holding of a ballot amongst the workers comprised in the relevant unit. The parties who may apply are:

1. The employer.
2. The organisation of workers, provided that at the time it makes the application it is a trade union, i.e. a body registered with the Registrar of Trade Unions set up under the Act. This, of course, is the sting in the tail. An unregistered organisation of workers may be recommended by the C.I.R. as sole bargaining agent, but before that organisation can apply to N.I.R.C. for an order establishing it as sole bargaining agent, it has to comply with the provisions of the Act covering registration.

Once application has been made to N.I.R.C., it makes arrangements with the C.I.R. for the holding of a ballot among the workers comprised in the unit on the question of whether or not they want this particular organisation as their bargaining agent. Voting is by secret ballot. If the voting is in favour of the organisation, N.I.R.C. will make an order directing that that trade union be recognised as sole bargaining agent for that bargaining unit. Where such an order is in force, then, by virtue of Section 55 of the Act, it is an unfair industrial practice for the employer to carry on any collective bargaining in relation to that bargaining unit with any other organisation of workers. Further, he has a duty to take all such action with a view

74

to carrying on collective bargaining with that trade union as might reasonably be expected to be taken by an employer 'ready and willing to carry on such collective bargaining'.

It is an unfair industrial practice for any person or organisation knowingly to threaten industrial action which has the aim of preventing the employer from carrying out his duties under Section 55.

DISCLOSURE OF INFORMATION

It seems axiomatic to this author that a voluntary system of collective bargaining can only operate successfully when both sides can freely communicate with each other. In Section 56 of the Act, a general duty to disclose certain information is imposed upon employers. It is worth setting out part of Section 56 in full:

(1) For the purposes of all the stages of collective bargaining between an employer and trade union representatives it shall . . . be the duty of the employer to disclose to those representatives all such information relating to his undertaking as is in the possession of the employer, or of any associated employer, and is both:

(a) information without which the trade union representatives would be to a material extent impeded in carrying on collective bargaining with him; and

(b) information which it would be in accordance with good industrial relations practice that the employer should disclose to them for purposes of collective bargaining.

In deciding what would be in accordance with good industrial relations practice, regard is to be had to those provisions of the Code of Practice dealing with disclosure of information by employers. At present this is dealt with in paragraphs 51 to 70 of the Code. Here the requirements are so broadly stated as to be of little use. Matters these set out include the desirability of discussions prior to the introduction of new plant and processes and the importance of close management and worker representative contacts.

Section 158 grants an immunity against the disclosure of certain confidential information. This includes:

1. The disclosure of any information which would be against the interests of national security.

2. Any information communicated to the employer in confidence.
3. Any information relating specifically to an individual (unless he consents to its being disclosed).
4. The disclosure of any information which would be seriously prejudicial to the interests of the employer's undertaking for reasons other than its effect on collective bargaining.
5. Any information obtained by the employer for the purpose of bringing or defending any legal proceedings.

Any employer having an undertaking which employs more than 350 people must issue a report to the employees of that concern in respect of each financial year. The report must be in writing and must be given to each employee. The information required to be given may extend to information about other undertakings owned by the company and to the undertakings of associated companies (see Section 57).

Finally, it should be noted that Section 58 empowers the Secretary of State to make regulations requiring employers to inform the Secretary of State whether they are parties to any procedure agreement and to furnish a copy of such agreement to him. Non-compliance with such regulations is a criminal offence.

Index of Cases

Index of Statutes